roots for kids

A Genealogy Guide for Young People

Susan Provost Beller

BETTERWAY PUBLICATIONS, INC.
WHITE HALL, VIRGINIA

Published by Betterway Publications, Inc.
Box 219
Crozet, VA 22932

Cover design, photograph, and illustrations by Susan Riley
Typography by East Coast Typography, Inc.

Library of Congress Cataloging-in-Publication Data

Beller, Susan Provost
    Roots for Kids

    Bibliography: p.
    Includes index.
    Summary: An introduction to genealogy with instructions
on how to use sources at home and do research at local,
state, and national levels.
    I. Genealogy — Juvenile literature.   [1. Genealogy]
I. Title.
CS15.5.B45   1989   929′.1′072   88-35134
ISBN 1-55870-112-5

Printed in the United States of America
0987654321

*This book is dedicated to my husband, W. Michael
Beller, who always said I should write it,
to my three children, Michael Patrick, Jennie, and
Sean, who grew up thinking that everyone had
their picnics in cemeteries,
and to all those Beller and Provost ancestors
whose "stories" made genealogy impossible to resist.*

Acknowledgments

There are many people who have assisted in making this book a reality. Through the years, as I adapted material to use to teach kids how to do research and complained about how little was available, my husband continually encouraged me to write this book. Finally, while taking a course taught by Dr. Helene Lang at the University of Vermont, my opportunity arose with the assignment of a final project of my choice. When I approached her with the idea of beginning my book, she was supportive and enthusiastic.

My son, Michael Patrick, labored long and hard at what he frequently reminded me was an inadequate computer to type my scribbles into readable form. My husband, Michael, diligently edited the first draft. Several people who read the manuscript deserve thanks for their suggestions: my parents, Edward and Lauretta Provost; my brother-in-law, Daniel Beller, who read closely enough to catch the page where four lines had mysteriously disappeared; the assistant principal at Bristol Elementary School, Phoebe Barash, who took the time to assess the readability and appropriateness of the material; my friend and colleague, Chris Heath, who brought her teaching experience to her evaluation; and Mary Dearborn, a sixth grader who had taken my genealogy course the previous year.

Both of my small enrichment classes at Bristol Elementary School who served as subjects for the field testing of the ideas in final form deserve my thanks: Mary Dearborn, Suzannah Lathrop, P. J. Cousino, Ben Potter, Sarah Burpee, Kristen Way, Adam Heath, Chris Eling, Tim Bouvier, Steve McEvoy, Jaime Brassard, Pete Jackman, and Matt Norse. My thanks also to Tari Shattuck, the Gifted/Talented Coordinator the first year the class was held, for her encouragement and support, and to Terrance Evarts, Principal of Bristol Elementary School, for letting me take six kids on that first trip to Montpelier to see how they would do at adult research.

My thanks also to Hilary Swinson, my editor, whose review of the manuscript made it much more readable.

Preface

In April 1987, I had the pleasure of taking my genealogy enrichment class of six students to Vital Records and the Vermont Historical Society Library in Montpelier, Vermont. Over the years I had given many mini genealogy sessions to stir up kids' interest in genealogy, and to have them create a pedigree chart based on sources of information from relatives. I had also taught nine different genealogy courses for adults at various times. However, this was the first time I had done a complete course for kids, including two field trips to use the available resources. The people I had approached about bringing in six fourth to sixth graders had been somewhat reluctant. As the morning of our eagerly awaited visit dawned, I was also having my doubts.

Throughout the day a steady stream of visitors came to observe these "kids" doing genealogy. They were serious about their research. They were knowledgeable about the materials they were using. They handled materials with the proper respect and care. The day was a fantastic success for everyone involved.

The course had been difficult to prepare due to a lack of materials at a level appropriate for the young reader. That need led directly to this book. It is an attempt to transfer my twelve-week class onto paper — field trips and all. Each chapter represents one forty-five minute class session with homework assignments and class handout information included.

This material can be used in three ways:

1. As a twelve-week enrichment class in genealogy for grades four and up.

2. As a four to five week mini course in which students create a family tree based on home sources of information. Many social studies teachers have their students create a family tree, and this book offers a methodical introduction for best achieving the desired results.

3. As a self-taught genealogy course for grades six and up. A student user can work through the course one lesson at a

time, developing his or her own family tree and continuing research into locally available records.

I hope that from this book the students will obtain an understanding of and an interest in genealogical research. It is also my firm hope that each will decide to find the stories hiding in his or her own history.

Contents

An Introduction to Genealogy

Have you ever done one of those really big jigsaw puzzles — the kind with about a zillion pieces? If you have, you know that each of the pieces of the puzzle doesn't give you much of the picture. You can tell that a certain piece is part of the sky or the ground or the snow on the mountain. But it's only as you start to put all the pieces together and the whole picture takes shape that you can really see what the little pieces mean.

Genealogy is like a big jigsaw puzzle with a lot of the pieces missing. Tracing your family tree can help you put together a whole picture of your ancestors, your history, and your family's history. It's not always easy; sometimes too many of the pieces are missing. But it is like a jigsaw puzzle. You find yourself at work looking for one more piece that will put the whole picture together.

Genealogy is a way of finding out about the people who came before us. It is the stories of the lives of real people who lived in real places in earlier times. Geneal-

ogy is part history because our ancestors (the people we are descended from) lived a part of history. They fought in wars, were pioneers, or came over to American as Pilgrims. Or maybe they were Irish immigrants who fled the potato famine. Genealogy is mostly biography — the story of a person's life. It is also part detective story because we have to find clues about the people who lived so long ago. But most of all, genealogy is fun!

A Collection of Stories

One way to think of genealogy is as a collection of stories. Each person on your family tree is a story waiting to be told. No matter what that person did in his life, he has a story to tell. This book will help you discover how to find those stories. Some of the stories will be very dull, but most of them are really interesting. You may be surprised to find out all the great things your ancestors did in their lifetimes. Some of the stories are also a lot of fun. One example is a story of a relative of my husband. This man has been dead for over seventy years but his story is remembered to this day. He was famous as a kid for his Halloween pranks. One Halloween he and some friends managed to coax the neighbor's cow up onto the roof of a barn. It took most of the townspeople most of the next day to get the poor cow back down!

When I go into a school to give a guest talk about genealogy, I start by writing HISTORY on the chalkboard. Then I cross out the HI to show that history is made up of stories. There is one special story I like to tell that shows the difference between history stories and genealogy stories.

On May 15, 1864 in New Market, Virginia, there was a small Civil War battle. It wasn't a very important battle — you won't even find it mentioned in your social studies textbook. But it was different from other Civil War battles in one way. The Union troops were trying to sneak down the Shenandoah Valley to cut off Richmond (the Confederate capital) from the rest of the South. They had tried this several times and had always been stopped. This time, the Confederate General Breckinridge knew he needed more men and had to get them fast. So on his way up the valley, he stopped in Lexington, Virginia at the Virginia Military Institute (a preparatory school for boys) and recruited a group of VMI cadets to use as reserve troops. These were just boys, some as young as twelve years old. When the armies clashed at New Market, his troops were getting beaten. Right at the center of the lines, a gap opened up where the Confederates were being slaughtered. The line started to collapse. He had no troops to send in except the VMI cadets, so he finally

gave them the order to attack. They fought bravely and turned the tide of battle to the Confederate side, stopping the Union advance. VMI is still a military school today. Every year on May 15th, the anniversary of the battle, the roll of the 258 cadets who served in that battle is called. For ten of those names, the answer is "Dead on the field of honor." This story (which comes from *The Battle of New Market*, by William C. Davis, Doubleday and Company, Inc., 1975) is part of our history. It is the story of real people fighting a battle at a real place at a real time, and of some of those people dying in that battle. If your great-grandfather was one of those VMI cadets and saw his friends die on that field, or if your great-grandfather was a Union soldier who watched those boys march forward and fight, then that story is also part of your genealogy — your own stories of your ancestors.

I want to share just a few of the stories I have found in researching my genealogy, just to get you interested in finding your own. A few years ago, I was reading the legend of Casey Jones, the train engineer, to some of my third grade students. One of the children told me he didn't like the story because no engineer would give his life just to stop the train so the passengers wouldn't be killed. The next week I brought in a copy of an old newspaper article about Daniel Lyons, my husband's great-grandfather, who lost his life in a similar incident.

Daniel Lyons was born in County Cork, Ireland on February 12, 1855, one of nine children of shoemaker John Lyons and Mary McGregor. Everyone in Ireland was very poor, and the Lyons children wanted to come to America to make their fortunes. The oldest boy, John, stayed in Ireland with his parents to help his father run the cobbler shop. The others took a ship to America. When they got there, three of the brothers, Robert, Patrick, and Daniel, went to work laying railroad track. They worked hard and eventually all three became railroad engineers. They lived in Springfield, Missouri. Daniel made all of his own furniture for his family, and bought land and built houses on it. But his real love was music, and he spent hours playing his violin. His daughter Josephine, then fourteen, played the piano very well and planned to become a concert pianist. Daniel had found America to be a great place to live. One night when Daniel was driving his train, he noticed the front wheel on one side seemed loose. He told the station manager about it, and asked that it be fixed right away because he thought it might come off. The next night he asked if it had been fixed and was told it had, so he took out his train. He was near the small town of Weaubleau, Missouri when the wheel came off. He had two choices: to jump and try to save himself or stay with the train to slow it down with the hand brakes. He decided to stay with the train. Only two people died in the train wreck that night: Daniel Lyons and Henry C. Fox, the fireman on the train.

Not all the stories are sad, of course. I always bring to my first class a baby's christening dress. It's not the prettiest christening gown ever made, and some of the sewing isn't very well done. But it was made by a woman for her baby over a hundred years ago. This dress (along with the story after this one) is the thing that really got me started on genealogy so many years ago. The woman who made the dress was a Mohawk Indian living in a one-room cabin in the Canadian backwoods. She did all the stitching on the dress by firelight. That one-room home seemed great to her — she had grown up in an Indian longhouse. The dress has been passed down through the women of the family and eventually came to my father's sister for her daughter to wear. Because her daughter had no daughters, the dress then came to my daughter for her christening. When I first held that dress, I knew I had to find out more about this woman's story.

The second story that started me on genealogy was from my husband's family — a great adventure story about a man who hid in a coffin so the Confederate soldiers wouldn't kill him during the Civil War. James Wilson Beller lived in Charles Town, Virginia (now West Virginia) before the Civil War. In 1844 he started his own newspaper, the *Spirit of Jefferson*, which is still published today. He was a strong Confederate supporter. Because he supported the Confederates, he probably actually hid in a coffin to avoid being killed by Union troops. I don't know if this story is true, but when the *Spirit of Jefferson* published a special issue on September 20, 1957 to celebrate the fact that Jefferson County, West Virginia was 150 years old, they wrote about "a vindictive raid by Northern troops" during the Civil War. Their printing presses were damaged in the raid, and they could not publish the paper for six months.

One last story and I'll tell you how to start looking for your own stories. This story involves the only ancestor I have whose name is in the history books — one Martin Prevost who came to Quebec over three hundred years ago. In 1644 he married Marie-Olivier Silvestre Manitouabewich, a Huron Indian woman. Marie's father was an Indian scout. He worked with a fur trader named Olivier LeTardif and they became friends. When Marie was ten years old, her father asked his French friend to adopt her so she could be brought up as a French girl. She lived with the French people from then on. Martin and Marie's marriage was the first marriage recorded in what is now Canada between a white man and an Indian woman.

Finding Your Own Stories

Every family has its own stories. You may find someone very famous among your ancestors, or all your stories may be about regular, everyday people. You will find people who have done very good things in their lives. You may also find people who have done very bad things. The idea behind finding your ancestors and the stories is not to find someone great. The important thing is to find all those normal everyday people who make up your past.

I once had a client (a person who pays me to find information about his or her family) who wanted very much to believe that he was descended from George Washington, and asked me to prove it. I had to tell him that George Washington did not have any children. The two children he raised were his wife's children from her first marriage. This man was very angry with me because I could not prove his relationship.

What that man forgot, and what you must not forget, is that every single person who has ever lived has been an important part of history. Maybe not important to

the whole world, but every person is important to his family and to the people who come after him. So don't worry if the people you find in your past are not famous or rich or kings. Without them, you would not even be here! And that makes them important for you and your research.

Genealogy as History

One thing is important to remember when you are doing genealogical research. Genealogy is history — a story of real people who lived in real places at real times in history. All good genealogists try to do their research carefully without making mistakes. We all do make some, but we TRY to make as few as possible. There are two reasons for this. The first is that, because genealogy is history, you want other people to know that your work is true. That way they will not have to redo everything you do. That's why it's so important to write down very carefully every piece of information you find and where you found it.

The second reason for not making mistakes is that genealogical research builds on what you have already done. So if you make a mistake and write down the wrong person for your great-grandfather, when you finally realize you've made a mistake, all the work done since will be useless. That can be very frustrating.

How this Book Works

When you do genealogical research, you start out with the things you know. When you run out of information from your own family, you go to your parents' families.

You just keep moving back in time further and further.

In the next chapter we will start with information about you and your immediate family. Then we add your parents' families and learn how to ask the right questions. Only when we've spent a long time on the answers you can find at home or from relatives do we move on to official records.

With official records we start with local records for births, marriages, and deaths, and then talk about land and will records. Then we discuss state records, and finally we talk about national records such as census and military records.

When we run out of official records, we talk about all the other places you can go to find information — libraries and historical societies, cemeteries, church records, and old newspapers.

Genealogy is lots of fun, but there are some things you need to know before you get started. It's important that you not try to understand it all at once, but take it one step at a time. And when we've finished, you'll be surprised at how much you will know.

Getting Started

By now you are ready to start finding your own stories of the past. Before you begin the next chapter you need the following information:

1. Your full name
2. Your birth date and exact place of birth
3. Your brother(s) and sister(s) full names
4. Your brother(s) and sister(s) birth dates and places of birth
5. Your parents' full names
6. Your parents' dates and places of birth and date and place of marriage

One good way to get this information is to ask your parents for the birth certificates of everybody in your family.

You and Your Family

With this chapter you begin looking for your own stories of the real people in your past. We need to start by learning about some of the information you should find out about people. We also need to find out the meanings of some of the words you will be using and a way to write down the information so you will be able to find it easily and not lose any of it. The next two chapters cover all these details of genealogy.

What Information Do You Need?

Genealogists start their work with three pieces of information for each of their ancestors: the date and place of birth, marriage, and death. These three facts are the ones which mark the most important events in most people's lives. The records containing these facts are called vital records. Later in this chapter we will look at what these records include. Then, in Chapter 6, we will discuss how to find and use vital records that you do not have copies of in your family.

We will always be looking for births, marriages, and deaths. But there is other information that we usually look for to make our records complete such as the name of the church the person attends, his occupation, and any military service. We also write down if they were married at any other time. It is not unusual to have people with two or three other marriages listed. Usually the one you list on your family group sheet is the set of parents, grandparents, etc. from whom you are descended. The others you can list on the back of your form. We will be talking about how to put your information onto family group sheets soon. But first, let's define some genealogical terms.

Definitions

Paternal — Your father's family line; your paternal grandfather is your father's father.

Family Group Sheet Number: _16_

Husband: BELLER, Ephraim S.

	Date	Place	Source
Birth:			
Marriage:	30 May 1816	Jefferson Cty, W. Va.	m. cert.
Death:			
Occupation:	Cabinetmaker	Military Service: War of 1812	
Church:	Methodist	Other Marriages: no	
Father:	Peter Beller	Mother: Amelia Sagathy	

Wife: REED, Sarah

	Date	Place	Source
Birth:	1793	Charlestown, Jeff Cty, W. Va.	Census
Marriage:	30 May 1816	Jefferson Cty, W. Va.	m. cert.
Death:	14 May 1870	Charlestown, Jeff Cty, W. Va.	d. cert.
Occupation:	Homemaker		
Church:	Methodist	Other Marriages:	
Father:		Mother:	

Children (Start with oldest):

Name	Birth	Marriage	Spouse	Death
James Wilson	1 Jun 1819 West Virginia	17 Feb 1848 Charlestown no m. cert. — newspaper notice	Jane Elizabeth Kelly	22 Oct 1877 Charlestown no d.cert.; obituary bur: Edge Hill Cem.
Amelia R.	1823	none	none	1 Jan 1875 Charlestown, W. Va. d. cert.: age 52, pneumonia
John M.	1827	none	none	20 Jan 1873 Charlestown, W. Va. d. cert.: age 46, printer
Charles Edward	Dec 1834 Charlestown, W. Va.	2 Apr 1857 Winchester, VA m. cert.	Ella Virginia Haines	9 Mar 1909 Washington, DC d. cert. bur: Edge Hill Cem.

Maternal — Your mother's family line; your maternal grandfather is your mother's father.

Spouse — Husband or wife.

Family Group Sheet — A record that has one whole family on it with all the information in one place.

Vital Records — A record of birth, marriage, or death.

Pedigree Chart — A chart showing all of your ancestors without the other members of their families. See Chapter 3 for a detailed explanation.

Generation — Each full family group is one generation. You count as the first generation, so a five generation pedigree chart has you, your parents as second generation, your grandparents as third generation, your great-grandparents as fourth generation, and your great-great-grandparents as fifth generation.

Occupation — A person's career or work in life.

Document — An official certificate or other written-down information saying that something is true under law. A birth, marriage, or death certificate is a document. To document something means to show from which official source you took your information.

Deed — A record of the transfer of a piece of real property (land or a house) from one person to another. See Chapter 7 for more information.

Will or Probate Records — Records used to distribute everything that a person owns at his death. See Chapter 7 for more information.

Abstract — A short form of a deed or will record that keeps only the important genealogical information.

Family Group Sheets

Many different companies print family group sheets that you can buy. But most of them are complicated and hard to use for someone just starting out doing a family tree. So I have included a simple one that you can use to get started. You can make copies of this or you can take some looseleaf paper and copy down the information you will need for each family group.

A family group sheet is where you list all the information you can find about one family. I usually keep my stories or pictures of that same family on looseleaf pages right after the family group sheet. On the group sheet you put those three pieces of information (birth, marriage, and death) about each person. All the information here is the kind you get from public records. You should always write down where you found the information so you can go back and look at it again if you have to.

Parts of the Family Group Sheet

Look at the sample family group sheet. (A blank sheet for your use is included in the back of the book.) Notice the kinds of important information I have included.

1. Husband's full name; dates and places of birth, marriage, and death; occupation; military service; church membership; any other marriages; and his parents' names.

2. Wife's full maiden name; dates and places of birth and death; occupation; church membership; any other marriages; and her parents' names.

3. For each child — name; dates and

places of birth, marriage, and death; name of spouse.

4. A place to list sources of information for the husband and wife. Sources on children can be listed with this information.

Documenting

If you use a birth, marriage, or death certificate, write down b. cert or m. cert or d. cert in the source column. Include the volume and page number if there is one.

If you find your information in a family Bible write BIBLE. Then, on the back of the sheet, write FAMILY BIBLE, currently owned by [name and address]. If you use a family Bible it's a good idea to photocopy all of the listings since you might not get to see it often.

If you find your information in a census or military record, include all the information on the back of your sheet or on a separate piece of paper after it.

If you find your information in a book, write down all the information about the book so you can find it again if you need to. Include the library or collection you saw it in, along with the other bibliographic data: title, author, publisher, copyright date.

Birth Certificate

Look at the sample birth certificate on the next page. This is a copy of an official standard certificate. Old birth records sometimes gave very little information. These new ones are more complete. Most states now use one like this. Let's look at some of the information you can use from this.

Child:

Name (some will just say "baby boy" or "baby girl" if the parents did not select a name before the record was filed)

Date and time of birth

Place of birth

Mother:

Full maiden name

Age

Her place of birth (state or country)

Father:

Full name

Age

His place of birth (state or country)

The rest of the information is used by the state health department. This part does not appear in the records you get at the vital records office.

Marriage Certificate

Look at the sample marriage certificate on page 22. This is a copy of an official standard marriage certificate. Very old marriage records usually gave only the names of the bride and groom and the date of their marriage. Then the names of their parents were added. That really helped because then you can add another whole family to your pedigree chart.

The information given today can really help in your research. Here is a list of some of the important information.

Groom:

Full name

Where he lives

State and date of birth — with these two pieces of information you can try to get his birth certificate

Father's name and state of birth

Mother's maiden name and state of birth

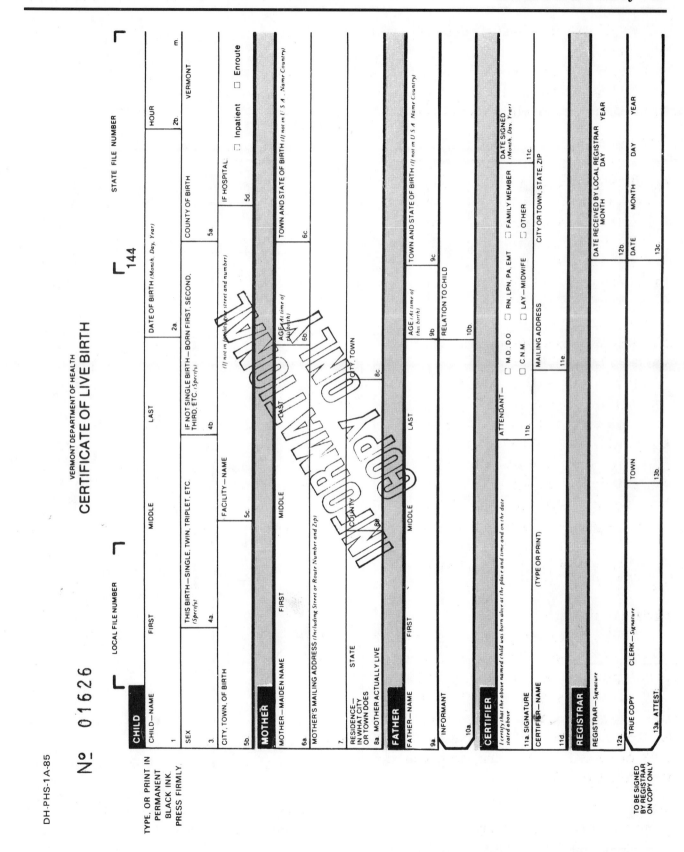

DH-PHS-1A-85

№ 01626

VERMONT DEPARTMENT OF HEALTH
CERTIFICATE OF LIVE BIRTH

LOCAL FILE NUMBER

STATE FILE NUMBER

Γ 144

TYPE, OR PRINT IN PERMANENT BLACK INK. PRESS FIRMLY

CHILD

CHILD—NAME FIRST MIDDLE LAST DATE OF BIRTH *(Month, Day, Year)* HOUR
1 2a 2b

SEX THIS BIRTH—SINGLE, TWIN, TRIPLET, ETC. *(Specify)* IF NOT SINGLE BIRTH—BORN FIRST, SECOND, THIRD, ETC. *(Specify)* COUNTY OF BIRTH VERMONT
3 4a. 4b 5a

CITY, TOWN, OF BIRTH FACILITY—NAME IF HOSPITAL ☐ Inpatient ☐ Enroute
5b. 5c. 5d

MOTHER

MOTHER—MAIDEN NAME FIRST MIDDLE LAST AGE *(At time of this birth)* TOWN AND STATE OF BIRTH *(If not in U.S.A. Name Country)*
6a 6b 6c

MOTHER'S MAILING ADDRESS *(Including Street or Route Number and Zip)* *(If not in city apply street and number)*
7

RESIDENCE— IN WHAT CITY OR TOWN DOES STATE COUNTY CITY, TOWN
8a MOTHER ACTUALLY LIVE 8b. 8c.

FATHER

FATHER—NAME FIRST MIDDLE LAST AGE *(At time of this birth)* TOWN AND STATE OF BIRTH *(If not in U.S.A. Name Country)*
9a 9b 9c

INFORMANT RELATION TO CHILD
10a 10b

CERTIFIER

I certify that the above named child was born alive at the place and time and on the date stated above ATTENDANT— ☐ M.D., DO ☐ RN, LPN, PA, EMT ☐ FAMILY MEMBER DATE SIGNED *(Month, Day, Year)*
☐ CNM ☐ LAY—MIDWIFE ☐ OTHER
11a. SIGNATURE 11b. 11c.

CERTIFIER—NAME *(TYPE OR PRINT)* MAILING ADDRESS CITY OR TOWN, STATE, ZIP
11d 11e

REGISTRAR

REGISTRAR—Signature DATE RECEIVED BY LOCAL REGISTRAR MONTH DAY YEAR
12a 12b

TO BE SIGNED BY REGISTRAR ON COPY ONLY TRUE COPY CLERK—Signature TOWN DATE MONTH DAY YEAR
13a. ATTEST: 13b 13c

DH-PHS-9-83

LOCAL FILE NUMBER

VERMONT DEPARTMENT OF HEALTH
CERTIFICATE OF MARRIAGE
(DECLARATION OF INTENTION AND MARRIAGE CERTIFICATE)

STATE FILE NUMBER

TYPE OR PRINT IN PERMANENT **BLACK INK PRESS FIRMLY**

41059

GROOM

1 NAME — FIRST — MIDDLE — LAST

2 MAILING ADDRESS — STREET OR R.F.D. — CITY/TOWN — STATE — ZIP

3 RESIDENCE — STATE — 3A IN WHAT CITY OR TOWN DOES — 3B COUNTY — 3C CITY, TOWN
3 GROOM ACTUALLY LIVE

4A DATE OF BIRTH (Month, Day, Year)

4B STATE OF BIRTH (If not in U.S.A. Name Country)

5 FATHER—Full Name — 5A STATE OF BIRTH (If not in U.S.A. Name Country) — 5B

6 MOTHER—Full Maiden Name — 6A STATE OF BIRTH (If not in U.S.A. Name Country) — 6B

BRIDE

7 NAME — FIRST — MIDDLE — LAST

7A MAILING ADDRESS — STREET OR R.F.D. — CITY/TOWN — STATE — 7B ZIP

8 RESIDENCE — STATE — 8A IN WHAT CITY OR TOWN DOES — COUNTY — CITY/TOWN
8 BRIDE ACTUALLY LIVE

9A DATE OF BIRTH (Month, Day, Year)

9C

10A STATE OF BIRTH (If not in U.S.A. Name Country) — 10B

11 FATHER—Full Name — 11A STATE OF BIRTH (If not in U.S.A. Name Country) — 11B

12 MOTHER—Full Maiden Name — 12A MAIDEN NAME—(If different) — STATE OF BIRTH (If not in U.S.A. Name Country) — 12B

APPLICANT

WE HEREBY CERTIFY THAT THE INFORMATION PROVIDED IS CORRECT TO THE BEST OF OUR KNOWLEDGE AND BELIEF AND THAT WE ARE FREE TO MARRY UNDER THE LAWS OF VERMONT.

13A APPLICANT—Signature — 13B DATE SIGNED — 13C APPLICANT—Signature — 13D DATE SIGNED

CERTIFICATION:

I hereby certify that the above named persons have made oath to the truth of the facts stated in the foregoing declaration of intention of marriage and complied with the marriage laws of the State of Vermont. A medical certificate or waiver, as per 18 V.S.A. 5136-5137, is on file in this office.

14A DATE ON WHICH LICENSE WAS ISSUED — 14B TOWN OR CITY — 14C

14A TOWN CLERK—Signature — 14D CITY/TOWN AND COUNTY OF MARRIAGE:

THIS LICENSE IS VALID FROM _____ DATE _____ TO _____ DATE
UNLESS WAIVED BY A VERMONT COURT.

OFFICIANT

This license authorizes the marriage of the above named couple by any person duly authorized to perform a marriage ceremony. THIS LICENSE IS VALID ONLY IN VERMONT.

15A I CERTIFY THAT THE ABOVE PERSONS WERE MARRIED ON THIS DATE:

15B DATE SIGNED (Month, Day, Year)

15C OFFICIANT—Signature — 15D RELIGIOUS OR CIVIL OFFICIAL (Specify) — 15E

16A CLERK'S SIGNATURE — 16B DATE RECEIVED BY LOCAL REGISTRAR

17A TRUE COPY—Clerk Signature — Attest: — 17B TOWN — 17C DATE

INFORMATIONAL COPY ONLY

Bride:
Full name and maiden name (if different). This might give you a clue that she was married before.
Where she lives
State and date of birth
Father's name and state of birth
Mother's maiden name and state of birth

You can see that if you don't know anything else about this couple, you can find a lot of useful information on the marriage certificate. You would now be able to request each of their birth certificates. You would have their parents' names and places of birth, so you could start looking for their birth certificates. This one record could give you many ideas of places to go for more information.

Death Certificate

Look at the sample death certificate on page 24. This is again the standard official death record used in most states today. Early death records gave almost as much information. Usually they contained the person's name, date of death, cause of death, the person's age, name of husband or wife, and occupation. Today the records also ask for the names of the person's parents (but no state of birth for them). It

does request the person's date of birth and the state where he or she was born. With that information you might try to get a birth record. Much of the information on this form will not help you. What would be helpful is to write down the place of burial since that would lead you to cemetery records, possibly with more information.

Homework

Before we go on to Chapter 3, you need to actually do the work we've talked about in Chapter 2. Make a family group sheet for your immediate family like the sample one in this chapter. Fill in all of the information you can. Be sure to use full names and to document your information from actual records if you can.

For the next chapter you will need to get the same types of information on your parents' families:

The full names of your grandparents
Their dates and places of birth, marriage, and death (if necessary)
The full names of your grandparents' children
The children's dates and places of birth, marriage, and death (if necessary)
The names of the children's spouses

DH-PHS-5X-78

LOCAL FILE NUMBER

VERMONT DEPARTMENT OF HEALTH

COPY OF CERTIFICATE OF DEATH

STATE FILE NUMBER

DECEASED

1 DECEASED—NAME   FIRST   MIDDLE   LAST

2 SEX

3 DATE OF DEATH (Month, Day, Year)

4 RACE—(White, Black, American Indian, ETC. (Specify)   5A AGE LAST BIRTH-DAY (Years)   5B UNDER 1 YEAR   MOS   DAYS   5C UNDER 1 DAY   HOURS   MIN   6 DATE OF BIRTH (Month, Day, Year)   7A COUNTY OF DEATH

7B STATE OF BIRTH (If not in U.S.A. name country)   7C HOSPITAL OR OTHER INSTITUTION (If not in either, give Street and Number)   7D IF HOSPITAL or INSTITUTION   Inpat.   ER   DOA

8 CITY, TOWN OF DEATH   9 CITIZEN OF WHAT COUNTRY?   10 MARRIED, NEVER MARRIED, WIDOWED, DIVORCED (Specify)   11 SURVIVING SPOUSE (If wife, give maiden name)

12 SOCIAL SECURITY NO.   13A USUAL OCCUPATION (Give kind of work done during most of working life, even if retired)   13B BUSINESS OR INDUSTRY   14 VETERAN? (If so, what war?)

USUAL RESIDENCE WHERE DECEASED LIVED. IF DEATH OCCURRED IN INSTITUTION, GIVE RESIDENCE BEFORE ADMISSION

15 ACTUAL RESIDENCE   15A STATE   15B COUNTY   15C CITY, TOWN   15D MAILING ADDRESS, INC. ZIP

PARENTS

16 FATHER—NAME   FIRST   MIDDLE   LAST

17 MOTHER—MAIDEN NAME   FIRST   MIDDLE   LAST

18A INFORMANT—NAME   18B MAILING ADDRESS (Street; R.F.D. No., City or Town, State, Zip Code)

CAUSE

19 PART I. DEATH WAS CAUSED BY: APPROXIMATE INTERVAL BETWEEN ONSET AND DEATH

IMMEDIATE CAUSE   (A)

CONDITIONS, IF ANY, GIVING RISE TO THE IMMEDIATE CAUSE (A), STATING THE UNDERLYING CAUSE LAST   DUE TO, OR AS A CONSEQUENCE OF: (B)

DUE TO, OR AS A CONSEQUENCE OF: (C)

PART II. OTHER SIGNIFICANT CONDITIONS: Conditions contributing to death but not related to cause given in Part I (A)   [(Include only one condition per line for (A), (B), and (C)]

20A AUTOPSY   YES   NO   20B IF YES, WERE FINDINGS CONSIDERED IN DETERMINING CAUSE OF DEATH   YES   NO

21A Natural   Accident   Suicide
Homicide   Undet.   Pending

21B INJURY AT WORK (Specify Yes or No)   21C DATE OF INJURY (Month, Day, Year)   21D HOUR

21E PLACE OF INJURY At Home, Farm, Factory, Street, Office Bldg., etc. (Specify)   21F LOCATION   21G HOW DID INJURY OCCUR (Enter nature of injury in Part I or Part II)

19D HOSPITALIZED IN LAST 6 MONTHS?   YES   NO   19E SURGERY IN LAST 6 MONTHS?   YES   NO

LOCATION   (Street, or R.F.D. No., City or Town   State)

CERTIFIER

22A (Signature)   22B NAME & ADDRESS OF CERTIFIER (Type or Print)

23A DATE SIGNED (Mo., Day, Yr.)   23B HOUR OF DEATH

PRONOUNCED DEAD ON: (Date)   (Time)

Staff phys.
Attend. phys.
Pathologist
Med. Examiner

24 NAME OF ATTENDING PHYSICIAN IF OTHER THAN CERTIFIER (Type or Print)

BURIAL

25A BURIAL, CREMATION, REMOVAL (Specify)   25B CEMETERY OR CREMATORY—Name   25C LOCATION   (City or Town, State)

25D DATE (Month, Day, Year)   26A FUNERAL HOME—Name   (Street or R.F.D. No., City or Town, State, Zip Code)

26B FUNERAL DIRECTOR—Signature   27A REGISTRAR—Signature   27B DATE RECEIVED—By local registrar (Month, Day, Year)

(TO BE SIGNED BY REGISTRAR ON COPY ONLY)

28A TRUE COPY ATTEST: Clerk's Signature   28B TOWN OF   28C DATE   (Month, Day, Year)

INFORMATIONAL COPY ONLY

Your Parents' Families

As we begin Chapter 3, you will have filled in one family group sheet. By the end of this chapter, you will have filled in two more group sheets and will have started a pedigree chart.

There are some little things you can do to make all of your family group sheets look the same and to help you find information more quickly. These are:

1. Always put the family last name first and in capital letters for both the husband's and wife's names. Example: BELLER, Walter Michael. This really helps if you get a confusing name later on and can't remember which is first or last.

2. Always write out the full name if you know it, including the middle name.

3. For women, always use the full maiden name. That way you always have two full family lines on your sheet.

4. When you start doing genealogical research, you will find that most genealogists put the day before the month when they are writing a date. It is very impor-tant to pick one system and to use the same system all the time. Otherwise, when you see 6/5/1857 you won't know whether it is May 6, 1857 or June 5, 1857. Notice also that I wrote out 1857. Always write out the year because once you get going you'll be using 1600s, 1700s, 1800s, and 1900s, and you'll need to keep them straight. I use a simpler date system that prevents mixups. Put the day first but use a three-letter abbreviation for the month instead of using another number. So I would write 6 May 1857 or 5 Jun 1857. The abbreviations for the months are:

Jan – January	Jul – July
Feb – February	Aug – August
Mar – March	Sep – September
Apr – April	Oct – October
May – May	Nov – November
Jun – June	Dec – December

With this new information it's time to redo your first family group sheet using these rules. Check also as you copy it over that you have always written down your sources of information. You can look back at Chapter 2 at the filled-in family group sheet to make sure you have done everything correctly. At the top of your family group sheet where it says "Number" write down "2." I will explain why when we get to the pedigree chart.

Now it is time to take all of the information you have gotten on your parents' families and fill in two new group sheets: one with your father's father as head of the family (Family Group #4), and one with your mother's father as head of the family (Family Group #6).

As you start to fill in these two sheets, you are probably getting to the point where you do not have actual birth records to use. You might have a family Bible if you are lucky. You will want to fill in these blank spaces by using vital records.

Pedigree Charts

A pedigree chart is a way of listing all of your ancestors on one form. You can see your family tree as it goes back and see the branching. The pedigree chart lets you see at a glance how far you have gone in your research. There are many kinds of pedigree charts. Some are made to look like trees with branches. Some are shaped like fans. The sample pedigree chart I have included is a simple, all-purpose chart to get you started. In the back of the book is a blank copy you can use to make copies for your own research. Also at the end of the book is also a list of companies who sell genealogy materials such as printed family group sheets and pedigree charts for nine or twelve or more generations. As your research goes further along, you will need a large pedigree chart of some kind to keep track of all your lines.

Some pedigree charts just give you room to list the names. Others list dates for the first few generations. Pedigree charts are easy to use and they help keep all your family group sheets in order. To make it easier, put last names in capital letters again so you'll always know which is which. I have taken a pedigree chart and filled in the name blanks with relationships (father, mother, grandfather, etc.) so you can see how easy it is. Study this sheet before we go on to discuss how it is numbered, which is the only tricky part to using these charts.

Numbering

If you look at the sample five-generation pedigree chart, you can see that you are number 1, your father is number 2, and your mother is number 3 on the chart. You can see that the male lines all have even numbers (2, 4, 6, 8, 10, 12, 14, 16, 18, 20, 22, 24, 26, 28, 30). The wives of each family group have odd numbers (3, 5, 7, 9, 11, 13, 15, 17, 19, 21, 23, 25, 27, 29, 31). The wife's number is always the number after her husband's number. For example, since your paternal grandfather is #4, your paternal grandmother must be #5.

Now comes the tricky part. Every generation doubles the number of the person in the generation before. The father of #4 is 4 x 2 or #8. The father of #12 is 12 x 2 or #24. The father of #15 is 15 x 2 or #30. And the neat thing about this system is that it goes on and on. The father of #20 is #40. The father of #40 is #80 and it keeps going. The biggest number on my pedigree chart is in the 30,000s, but it all comes from multiplying each generation

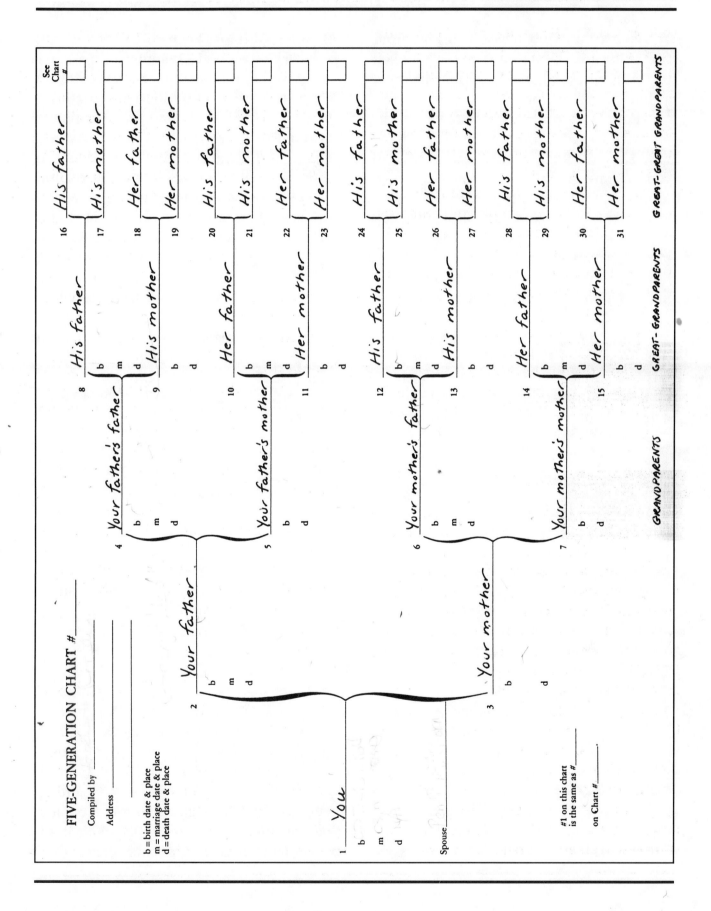

FIVE-GENERATION CHART # _____

Compiled by _____

Address _____

b = birth date & place
m = marriage date & place
d = death date & place

1 You
b
m
d

Spouse _____

#1 on this chart
is the same as # ____
on Chart # ____

2 Your Father
b
m
d

3 Your Mother
b
d

4 Your Father's Father
b
m
d

5 Your Father's Mother
b
d

6 Your Mother's Father
b
m
d

7 Your Mother's Mother
b
d

GRANDPARENTS

8 His Father
b
m
d

9 His Mother
b
d

10 Her Father
b
m
d

11 Her Mother
b
d

12 His Father
b
m
d

13 His Mother
b
d

14 Her Father
b
m
d

15 Her Mother
b
d

GREAT-GRANDPARENTS

See Chart #

16 His Father

17 His Mother

18 Her Father

19 Her Mother

20 His Father

21 His Mother

22 Her Father

23 Her Mother

24 His Father

25 His Mother

26 Her Father

27 Her Mother

28 His Father

29 His Mother

30 Her Father

31 Her Mother

GREAT-GREAT GRANDPARENTS

by two. If you find it confusing at first, that's okay. It takes some time to get used to. But as you get going, you'll be surprised at how easy it becomes.

Family group sheets are always written with the husband's name first. That's why they all have even numbers. So all your family group sheets will have even numbers, and you can just keep them in numerical order. No matter how far back you go, you don't need to change the system. There are some very complicated systems you will see in some books or in printed family histories, but most people try to keep it simple and easy to use.

Make a copy of the blank sample and put your name on line 1. Then put your father's name on line 2 and your mother's on line 3. Your father's parents go on lines 4 and 5. Your mother's parents go on lines 6 and 7. And just keep going.

One question I am sometimes asked is what you do if you are in a stepfamily. When you are researching, you usually use your own father and mother for lines 2 and 3. But there is no rule that says you can't add your stepfather's or stepmother's lines to your research. Remember, you are doing the research *you* are interested in.

Homework

You should finish copying information on family group sheets 4 and 6 at this time. You can also begin on sheets 8, 10, 12, and 14 just from information your parents can give you. In the next chapter we will discuss interviewing people to fill in answers on those new group sheets.

Asking Questions:
Genealogy as Oral History

You've been working on your family tree for some time now. You've looked at all the records your parents have at home. You've seen your birth certificate and those of your parents and brothers and sisters. You've seen your parents' marriage certificate. Your mother and father have given you as much information as they can remember about their parents and their brothers and sisters. You've recorded everything. You now have three family group sheets: 1) one for your own family with your father's name as head of it (FG#2); 2) one for your father's own family with your paternal grandfather's name as head of it (FG#4); and 3) one for your mother's own family with your maternal grandfather's name as head of it (FG#6).

So what's next? Now it's time to move out into the world and get some answers. The first step is to talk to other relatives — especially older relatives like grandparents and great-grandparents, great aunts and great uncles. These people who have lived so much longer than your parents have all sorts of information you need. But how do you begin? In this chapter we'll talk about who to ask, when to ask them, and most importantly, what to ask them. We'll also talk about how to ask and whether to take notes or tape record your conversations with them.

Who Should I Ask?

You should make a list of older relatives in your parents' families who might be able to answer your questions. Your grandparents are a great place to start. Start with someone you know — you might feel a bit silly asking all these questions at first. It's easier if the person is someone you know well. After you've exhausted the people you know, start with others you don't know as well. Remember that this is supposed to be fun. So if you have an older relative you don't feel comfortable with, don't start with that person.

When Do I Ask?

This is one of those really simple questions. But it is very important. You can't call your grandmother when she's busy making dinner and expect her to be happy to answer all your questions. You may need to set a special time for your interview. You want a time when you will not be disturbed. In the beginning you need to interview one person at a time. You also should not schedule a lengthy interview. Just plan on asking a few questions at first. Your parents can help by talking with relatives for you to help set up an interview. But remember, the research is yours. You shouldn't have your parents do the interviewing for you.

What Should I Ask?

Imagine that you did something that made you instantly famous. If someone came to interview you and said, "Tell me everything about you and your family," you wouldn't know what to answer. The question is too general. The situation is the same when you interview family members. The rule for asking questions is to make the questions simple enough that they can be easily answered.

Let's try to come up with a list of the kinds of questions that might be good to ask. We want questions that will give us our "stories." We want questions that will let people remember some of the special things that happened in their lives. Our questions should tell us what it was like to be a kid when they were growing up. (Remember the Halloween story I told you about earlier.) Finally, the questions should tell us about the people around the person being interviewed, so we can learn about them, too.

When I teach a genealogy class, we "brainstorm" questions so that each person has an emergency list of things to ask if they run out of their own questions. We start out with categories of questions: family, holidays, houses, pets, school, things (cars, favorite toys, TV, radio), and then put questions for each category. Listed here are some of the questions that I have brainstormed with kids in my classes:

Family:

How did you celebrate your birthday?

What kinds of things did the whole family do together — play games, listen to radio, etc.?

Did you have an older brother or sister take care of you? Did you have to take care of a younger brother or sister?

What's the favorite thing you remember about your mother when you were a child?

What's the favorite thing you remember about your father when you were a child?

Do you remember your grandparents? What were they like? Did you see them often?

Were you in the military? Which war, where were you stationed, what did you do?

Holidays:

What was the first thing you used to do on Christmas morning?

How did you decorate your Christmas tree?

What kinds of tricks did you play for Halloween?

What did you dress up as for Halloween?

What did you have for Thanksgiving dinner?

Did you have Thanksgiving dinner at home or at someone else's house? Who was there?

Did you celebrate New Year's Eve? How?

Did you dye Easter eggs? Did you have an Easter egg hunt or roll?

What special goodies did you have at special times of the year?

Did you have a Fourth of July parade? Fireworks?

What church did you go to?

Pets:

Did you have any pets? What kind? What color? What happened to them?

Favorite Things:

What was your favorite toy?

What was your favorite food? What foods did you NOT like?

Did you have a favorite place to go to be alone?

Did you have a place where you and your friends met (a treehouse, the corner drug store, etc.)?

What was your first car like?

What was the best present you ever received?

Tell me about dances and dates when you were a teenager. Where did you go?

What was your favorite vacation?

Houses:

Did you live in a city or in the country?

What was your house like (how many rooms, floors, etc.)?

Did you have your own bedroom?

What chores did you have to do at home?

Did you have a TV, radio, record player?

School:

What was your school building like?

How many people were in a class?

What was your favorite subject?

What did you like least about school?

Did you ever get in trouble in school?

Did you have a favorite teacher?

Did you go to a town library?

What were your favorite books?

What games did you play at recess?

What was the name of your best friend?

Asking Genealogy Questions

Of course, as much as you are enjoying all these stories, you are also supposed to be finding information for your family group sheets. So, in the middle of other questions, you can ask more specific questions. Don't ever ask only those because people get tired of them quickly. They also sometimes get upset because they can't remember the answers.

Some questions to ask:

When was your mother's birthday (month and day)?

When was your father's birthday (month and day)?

What were your brothers' and sisters' names?

What were your brothers' and sisters' birthdays?

Who did they marry? When (not date — just "when I was about twelve")? Where?

Do you remember your grandmother's and grandfather's names (one person at a time)? Where did he/she live? What time of year was his/her birthday?

Why Some of the Answers are Wrong

One of the most important things to

remember is that some of the answers will not be right. People forget things. They won't forget the stories, but they will forget the names and places and dates. Once I could not find a death record because everyone remembered that the person died in May when he actually had died in November.

You need to take the genealogical information you are given and check it with vital records or a family Bible or church records. But the stories you can just copy down to enjoy even if some of them are "tall" tales.

Remember also that the idea of the questions is to start people talking. You may find someone who will go from subject to subject and you won't have to say much at all. Another person may only answer the exact question you ask.

How to Interview

When you interview people, you can write down notes to remember what they said. But the best thing to do is use a tape recorder. Some people will not want to talk on a tape recorder, but many won't mind. You may have to start out taking notes. But then you might say, "Grandpa, I know you don't like the tape recorder, but I really would like to have your story about your first car in your own words. Could you tell just that one on tape?" He may say no, but he may say yes.

It is important that the people you are interviewing feel comfortable. I once tape recorded a very special conversation. My husband's grandmother, who was ninety-five years old, would not talk about the past. She was living in the future and thought the past was boring. One day I

asked her if I could tape her playing the piano, which she still did beautifully. That she would allow. Once she got used to the tape recorder, she started talking about how she learned to play the piano and then about her father. She died when she was ninety-nine years old, and that tape is fantastic to listen to now.

There are three more things I want to say here. The first is to do your questioning soon. There are lots of people I wish I could have taped. Many of their stories are lost forever.

The second thing is that you must remember to respect people's right to privacy. No one HAS to talk to you. If someone says no, that's okay. Don't make her feel bad — she may change her mind later. If someone will answer questions but won't let you tape or take notes, just remember the story as best you can and write it down when you get home. And very important, if someone tells you something and asks that you not tell someone else — always do what they ask. People will not talk to you if you do not respect their right to privacy.

The third and most important point of all — HAVE FUN! It's not important that you find all the answers — or even most of them. Try to find enough that you will have some great things to remember about the person. But keep in mind that you'll also want to remember later how much fun you had talking together. Once that person dies, the memory of that special time will mean even more than all the information you got from them.

Homework

Interview at least one person before going

on to the next chapter. Try to find information to fill in family group sheets #8, 10, 12, and 14, and get the names for the fifth generation on their pedigree charts. In Chapter 5, we will try to put all our research together. This will help us to get ready for our "field trips" in Chapters 8 and 12.

Putting It All Together

This chapter is the last of the "how-to" chapters for your genealogy. After this chapter, the remainder of this book is about different kinds of materials that can give us genealogical information. We'll also be talking about the places where this information can be found. From now on there is no special homework for each chapter. I will give you some advice for getting organized and continuing your work, and give you examples of ways to put things together.

What Do You Have?

If you have been following along with the homework assignments so far, you should have a pedigree chart with your own name, your parents' names, your grandparents' names, and hopefully, most of your great-grandparents' names filled in. The numbers on your pedigree chart stop at 31. For each even number beginning with number 2, you have a matching family group sheet. That means you have fif-

teen family group sheets numbered 2, 4, 6, 8, 10, 12, 14, 16, 18, 20, 22, 24, 26, 28, and 30. The group sheets are for the families shown in the chart on the following page.

At this point in your research, with a pedigree chart and fifteen family group sheets to work with, it is a good idea to get a looseleaf binder to keep it all in. Put the pedigree chart first and then put in all the family group sheets in numerical order from the lowest to the highest number. Now every time you get information about someone, you can add that information to the correct group sheet. If it is extra information — like a "story" for your collection — you can put it on a piece of looseleaf paper right after the family group sheet that lists that person. For example, when you talked to your maternal grandmother, she told a story about how her parents celebrated her birthday and those of her brothers and sisters. You should write that story on a piece of paper and put it behind group sheet #14 because it is about things that happened in that family.

Generation	FG#	Family	Head of Family
2	2	Your own family	Your father
3	4	Your father's family	Your father's father
	6	Your mother's family	Your mother's father
4	8		
	10	Your 4 grandparents' families	Your great-grandparents
	12		
	14		
5	16		
	18		
	20		
	22	Your 8 great-grandparents' families	Your great-great grandparents
	24		
	26		
	28		
	30		

What Do You Need?

Take the time now to put all your sheets in order as described above. Once you have done that, it is time to look at all the sheets and determine what information is missing. Start with FG#2 and go through it line by line, checking the information you have. Below is a list of questions to ask yourself as you check each one. Once you have been doing genealogical research for a while, you won't need a checklist like this. You will be able to tell what is missing just by glancing at your sheet. But for now, it is important to notice every part. So, with group sheet #2 in front of you, start answering these questions. Every time your answer to a question is "no," make a note to yourself of what is missing on a copy of the form in the back of the book. A sample list of missing information is on the form on the next page.

Remember that you do not need to do all this right now. My students do this over the course of two or three weeks. If you try to do it all at once, you'll probably get discouraged. It's better to take your time.

What to Do Next?

Now that you have checked over all of your family group sheets, it's time to decide where to go for your missing information. Notice that on the sample form I put in a column for "What to do now." I have filled in some suggestions for your sample page. Since each situation is different, it's hard to tell you where you should look next without seeing your actual information, but here are a few general rules to follow.

1. Try home sources first.

2. Always try to find vital records (births, marriages, and deaths) next; they are the easiest to track down.

3. If you are trying to put an old family group together, think of vital records

(Chapter 6), will records (Chapter 7), or census records (Chapter 10).

4. Once you know where a family lived, using land records can help you find out when and where they came there and/or when they left and where they went (Chapter 7). State and national censuses can help with this, too.

5. If the husband was in his late teens or twenties during wartime, check the military records — maybe you'll find him there (Chapter 10).

One important thing to keep in mind is that what you are learning to do in this chapter does not change, no matter how long you are involved in doing genealogical research. You will be constantly adding new information, putting it in place, and deciding what to look for next. As you do this, you will gradually move further and further back in your line of ancestors.

Remember also what I said in the beginning of Chapter 1. There are some answers you will never find, because the records you need to provide the information just don't exist anymore. You are putting the jigsaw puzzle of your ancestors together with only the pieces you happen to find. That's why genealogy can be very frustrating at times! But the fun comes in always searching, and in finding a piece of material you thought you'd never see.

Checklist

For husband do I have:

☐ Full name
☐ Birth date, place, and source
☐ Marriage date, place, and source
☐ Death date, place, and source
☐ Occupation
☐ Military service information
☐ Church attended
☐ Other marriages
☐ Father's name
☐ Mother's name

For wife do I have:

☐ Full maiden name
☐ Birth date, place, and source
☐ Death date, place, and source
☐ Occupation
☐ Church attended
☐ Other marriages
☐ Father's name
☐ Mother's name

For each child do I have:

☐ Full name
☐ Birth date, place, and source
☐ Marriage date, place, and source
☐ Name of spouse
☐ Death date, place, and source

Local Records:
Vital Records

In Chapters 1-5 we talked about using records that are available within your own family. We looked at the information given on a birth, marriage, or death record, and saw samples of them. Now that you have used up all of your family sources, it's time to talk about genealogical research outside of family information. For the rest of this book, we will discuss some of the major kinds of official records containing genealogical information. We will also talk about other sources of information: local histories, church records, and old newspapers. Some of the records I will discuss you will not be able to use, since only adults are allowed to visit some of the libraries or other places where genealogical information is located. We will talk about how to get permission and how to act if you do get the chance to visit.

We start out this chapter with the simplest of the genealogical information available outside the family — vital records. Since we've already talked about what information they have and why they

are important, what we will discuss here is how to find them and how to use them. We'll also come up with a sample letter you can use to write away for vital records, and talk about asking the kinds of questions that get answers.

Where Vital Records Are Kept

This chapter calls vital records "local records." These records are kept right in the communities where they occur — the towns, cities, or counties themselves. Copies of these records are also usually kept at some state offices. Vital records are the most important records for doing genealogical research. Unfortunately, for many years vital records were not kept. Births and deaths were not recorded regularly until after the Civil War, and in many states not until after 1900. In many of the cases where they were kept, they have not survived. Many records were destroyed in fires. Other records may have been destroyed by war, especially in Virginia counties during the Civil War. Many records have been destroyed by neglect. Some were written down on cheap paper that has fallen to pieces. Some clerks used ink that has faded so much that it cannot be read at all. I know of at least one county, and many people have told me of others, where old records are sitting in attics and being eaten up by rats. Because these are local records, with each individual jurisdiction (a jurisdiction is an area controlled by an official government, so you might have a town or a county or a state government) making its own decisions on how to care for its records, you will find great differences from place to place in the condition of the records. Some areas have complete records in perfect condition. In others you will find very little information.

In some states, a copy has been made of every single vital record in the smaller jurisdictions like towns or cities, and all the copies are available in one place. Vermont is one such state, and you can research all of Vermont's old vital records in one place in the state capital. Members of the Church of Jesus Christ of Latter-day Saints have tried to get permission to put all old local records on microfilm. This includes the vital records along with land, will, and court records. Most communities have allowed their records to be copied so that researchers can use them at any of the Church of Jesus Christ of Latter-day Saints genealogical libraries around the country. Other communities will not allow their records to be filmed.

Another point to keep in mind with these records is that they are not always accurate. I once found two different birth records for an ancestor I was researching.

Neither of them matched the birth date on his death record, which was the one his family said was right. Mistakes can be caused by a clerk taking down the information incorrectly — names especially can be a mess. Sometimes families registered all of their children's births at once, years after they were born. You must keep in mind that there are all sorts of weird surprises in the official records.

I am taking the time to show you the problems with vital records to make a point. The availability of vital records is very different from place to place. It is important that you find out what the situation is at your location before trying to do research. You don't want to be disappointed to find that the records are not there and feel you've wasted your time. It is also important to know that many of the places will not want students doing research, and if you don't seem to know what you're doing, they will not give you any chance at all.

There are two sources of information that you should become familiar with to help you find vital records. The first is a booklet published by the National Center for Health Statistics, U.S. Department of Health and Human Services. The booklet is called "Where to Write for Vital Records." It is available for $1.50 from the Superintendent of Documents, Government Printing Office, Washington, DC 20402. Be sure to ask for Publication No. 017-022-010089. This booklet is arranged by state, and for each state it gives information on where their birth, marriage, and death records are located. In the "Remarks" section, the pamphlet usually lists when the records begin for that state. The cost of obtaining a record is given, which saves you writing first to ask what the copies will cost. Buy this inexpensive booklet —it will help you in your research.

The second source to help you find vital records is called *The Handy Book for Genealogists* (7th edition, Logan, UT: Everton Publishers, Inc., 1981). It is an expensive book, but it is one that your public library may have if it has any genealogical collection at all. This book is arranged by state. For each state there is a short history, a list of names and addresses of genealogical libraries or organizations, a list of census records that have been printed in book form, a list of important material published about the state, a map of the state showing all the counties, and finally, information on how to get hold of local records. For each county, it gives the year it became a county, what census records (discussed in Chapter 10) are available for that county, what county it was formed from, where it is located (a mailing address), and a short description of the records located there and for which years they are available. For example, the listing for Jefferson County, West Virginia says: "Co Clk has b, d rec from 1853 (except CW years), m, pro, wills, lnd rec from 1801." (*Handy Book*, p. 314.) Translated, that means that the county has birth and death records beginning in 1853, but not those during the Civil War years (1860-65). The clerk has marriages, probate, wills, and land records beginning with 1801. As you can see, you can get a lot of necessary information before you even visit a place.

There is one problem with this book that you should know about. Each state is arranged by counties. That is fine for al-most every state in the U.S. But a few of them, including Vermont (where I live), do not use the county division for local records. In these states, everything to do with vital records and land records is handled by the towns or cities. *The Handy Book* tells you this, but does not give the information by town.

In Chapter 8 we will cover visiting a town or county clerk's office to do research, so I will not discuss that now. One part of research that I do need to cover is indexes to material at vital records. Many of the local clerks' offices have had their records indexed. This is a favorite project for local genealogical or historical societies. The indexes are then printed, and can be used just like the index to a regular book. Most of the local clerk's offices around the country have not had this done. Their records may have no index at all, or they may have a very different kind of index. I will tell you about the two that I have had to use. (A third index for land records will be discussed in the next chapter.)

The first kind of old index is the kind I have seen most often. In the front of the book where the births and deaths are recorded (many places have these two together in one book), there is a set of pages with alphabet tabs along the edges. When the clerk records a birth he or she turns to the correct letter of the alphabet and lists the name there along with the page on which the record can be found. So this is an index by first letter of last name only. In a thick vital records volume you might have to read through several hundred last names beginning with B to find the one you want. The book may also have two indexes if it has both birth and death records — one index for births and one for deaths.

The second kind of old index is like the first except it breaks the letters down further, so there might be pages for BA, BE, BI, BL, BR, and BU. Be careful with this kind, because the spelling of the clerks was not always accurate. I have found Beller spelled as Bellar, Baller, Ballar, Biller, Billew, and others. So with that kind of index, you still need to look at all the Bs. After a while you get really good at picking out your name on a page of names — even with the old-fashioned handwriting.

The lesson here is always to look through the book before you begin using it so that you understand its system and don't miss any information.

Writing for Vital Records

Let's suppose that you need your great-grandmother's birth certificate and you live in Massachusetts. You know your great-grandmother was born in California in 1886. Unless you are unusually lucky, you are not going to be able to run out and research wherever the records happen to be. Especially after your research starts to go far back, you will probably find that well over half of the people you are looking for did not live anywhere near where you are. So you have to start writing letters for information. The two sources I mentioned earlier, "Where to Write for Vital Records," and *The Handy Book*, will give you the addresses you need.

Let's talk about asking the questions to get the answers you want. Town clerks are often very busy people. If they get a letter asking for "everything you have on William Smith," they will send it back and say that they do not do genealogical research. You'll get the same kind of answer if you send a list of fifteen records you need copies of. But if you send the fee along with a nice clear letter asking for only two records and giving lots of information that will help their search, you will usually get an answer.

The most important part about getting an answer is to give the clerk enough information to find the person. It's important that you do as much as you can to find the person on your own first. Let's look at the kind of information you'd want to give to get each of the three kinds of vital records.

Birth:
  Full name
  Date of birth
  Place of birth
  Names of parents

Marriage:
  Full names of both bride and groom
  Date and place of marriage
  Names of their parents (if you know them)

Death:
  Full name
  Date and place of birth
  Date and place of death
  Names of parents and/or spouse

I realize that as you look at the list, your first thought is that if you knew all that stuff, you wouldn't need the record at all. But this is just here to get you started. Obviously, you won't know most of this, but it will help you provide as much information as possible, so that you stand a better chance of getting your answer. On the next page is a sample letter to write for a birth, marriage, or death record. You can use this, putting in your own information in place of mine to write for your records. You should never ask for more than two records at a time, as most places will not answer, but will refer you instead to a professional researcher. Always include a business-size envelope stamped and addressed to yourself (an SASE).

Homework

Look through the information you have already organized. Try to find a record that you can write away for and do so. Remember that in some places, especially big cities or state vital records offices, it may take up to six months to get an answer. Most smaller offices will answer within two or three weeks.

Note that I tried to write the request clearly and I put in all the information I had. For a death record, you might use the following example:

Death Record:
  William Smith
  Born 6 Sept 1873 (or 1874)
  Son of James and Margaret Smith
  Marriage in 1892 to Sarah Jones
  Died in 1925 (according to tombstone
      at Edge Hill Cemetery), (or, if you
      knew the date, 18 Oct 1925 in
      Harper's Ferry)

123 Main Street
Anytown, My State
April 1, 1989

County Clerk's Office
Jefferson City Courthouse
Charles Town, WV 25414

Dear Sir or Madam,

Enclosed is a check for $10 to obtain copies of the two following records:

Birth record:
        William Smith
        Born 8 Sept 1873 (or 1874)
        Son of James Smith and Margaret ?

Marriage record:

        William Smith
        Son of James and Margaret Smith
        Married ? 1892 Charles Town, West Virginia
                to
        Sarah Jones
        Daughter of WIlliam Jones and Mary Putnam

I am enclosing a self-addressed stamped envelope. Thank you for your help in this matter.

                Sincerely,

                My Name

Local Records:
Land and Will Records

In the last chapter we talked about vital records (births, marriages, and deaths) and how to find them. In this chapter we will discuss the other records which you can find locally. These include land records, will records, and court records. These records are not as easy to use as vital records, and they do not give as much information. But when the vital records are not available, either because the time period you are looking for is before the records were kept or because the records no longer exist, these can be a great help. I will explain how each type of record is kept, what information it contains, and how to use it. These are all complicated legal records and my explanation only tells a few things about them. I am just giving you an idea of when you might want to use them and what you will find if you do.

Land Records

There are two kinds of land records. One is the kind that gives the land to the first person ever to own it, when a state or territory was first settled. This type of record is called a land grant or a patent. These records go back to the beginnings of the colonies and then the states, when all the land was still owned by the state or national government. I will discuss this type in more detail in Chapter 9.

The other kind of land record is used when one owner gives the ownership of the land to another person. These are called deed records and they are kept in the town or county clerk's office. Before we talk about these records, there are some words you need to know.

Deed — The record made of the transfer of property from one person to another.

Real Property — Land and houses are "real" property. All other things we own that can move around with us are called personal property.

Grantor — The person selling the property.

Grantee — The person buying the property.

Witnesses — People who sign saying that these people are transferring the property willingly, that nobody is forcing them to do it.

When a piece of property is sold, the deed is recorded (written into the town record book) so that everyone will know it has been transferred. Towns have lots of legal reasons for doing this. One of them is so that the town can collect taxes from the correct owner. (All people who own property in a town pay a tax on the property to help pay for the cost of running the town.) Since deeds are important legal documents, most towns and counties have taken very good care of them. The deed books usually go all the way back to the beginning of a town or county.

Deeds do not make very interesting reading. They just give the names of the grantor and grantee, tell how much the property is being sold for, and give a legal description of the property. Some of the old legal descriptions can be fun to read, but they don't make much sense to us today. They talk about the property starting at the big oak tree and running by the line of pine trees to the large rock at the southeast corner. When you read some of these, you wonder how people were able to figure out where their property lines were at all.

Some of the important pieces of genealogical information in a deed can be taken out to save you from copying all the legal language you don't really want or need. This is called making an abstract of a deed, and it means keeping only the important information. You will want to find out the name of the grantor and where he or she lived, the name of the grantee and where he or she lived, the amount of the property (example: 400 acres and a house), the money paid for the property, the date of the sale, and the names of the witnesses. You will also want to list a reference for where you found the deed, like this: Jefferson County, West Virginia, Deed Book 12, p. 141. On the next two pages I have included a sample deed and a form showing how to make an abstract of a deed. A blank form for your use is in the back of the book.

Now the question is: "How can I use this information?" It does sound like lots of work for something that is not the most useful thing. However, deed records are important because 1) they place a person in a definite place at a definite time, 2) they can give you a person's occupation (farmer, storeowner, blacksmith, etc.), and 3) they were often used by parents to divide their property among their children (which gives you family relationships). A good example of this: I once had a person who was in all of the records in Berkeley County, West Virginia, and then just disappeared. I couldn't find him anymore. Then I found a deed where his wife was the grantor (the seller). She was selling a piece of property that she had received in her father's will after his death. The deed gave the place she lived as Warren County, Kentucky. Suddenly I had found where the family had gone, and I could trace them in those records.

One other point about deed records. Some of them have two indexes, one by grantor and one by grantee. If you only look for your ancestor in the grantor index, you will only find the times he sold

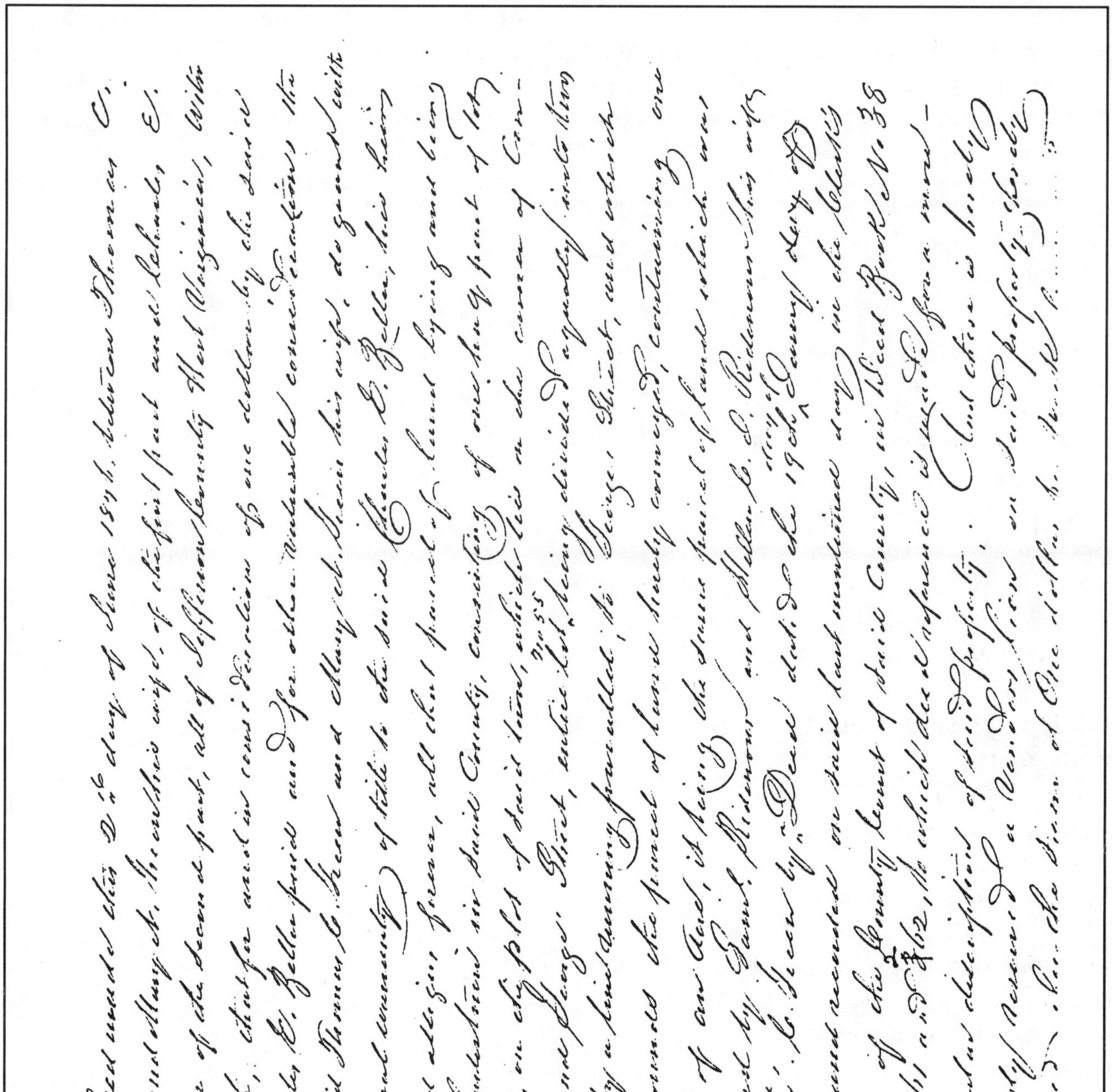

256

Abstract of Deed

County: *Jefferson, W. Va.*   Deed Book: *38*   Page: *256*

Name of Grantor: *Thomas C. and Mary N. Green*

Name of Grantee: *Charles E. Beller*

Description of Property: *"All that land lying and being in Charlestown in said county consisting of one ...? lot No. 55 on the plat of said town which lies on the corner of Congress and George Street, entire lot No. 55 being divided equally into two parts, by a line running parallel to George Street, and which line bounds the parcel of land hereby conveyed, containing one quarter of an acre..."*
24 Sep 1877

Amount Paid: *$1.00*

Witnesses: *can't read*

Legal Description of Property (if names included):

property, and you'll miss the times he bought property.

Remember that these are local records. You will find them at the same place as the vital records.

Will Records

When a person dies and has either real or personal property that he or she owns, that property has to be divided among the people who should get it (the heirs). Some people make a document before they die, called a will, that explains how they want the things they own divided up. If a person doesn't do this, then the government steps in to decide who should inherit what. The kinds of records that handle dividing up people's property after they die are called probate records. These are also local records. In places with counties, they are usually kept in the same place as the vital records and the land records. In places where the vital and land records are held by towns, the probate records are usually kept at the county clerk's office or by a special probate court.

If the person you are looking for died without a will, you usually will not get very much information from these records. But if the person left a will, you can sometimes get the whole family listed and get all kinds of useful information. The next page shows an abstract of a will for Jacob Beller to give you an example of how much you can find. As you can see, the entire family was listed here, including the daughter's married name and two grandsons' names.

To abstract a will you want to include the following information:

Name of the person making the will and the date and place it was made

Date and place the will was recorded (wills aren't recorded until after the person dies

Names of each of the persons mentioned and what they received

Name of the executor (the person in charge of doing what the will specifies)

Names of the witnesses to the will (these have to be people who are not receiving anything from the will).

In the back of this book is a blank form you can use to make abstracts from will records.

Court Records

The last kind of local record I want to mention here is court records. When people disagree on who owns something or on other matters, their disagreements are often settled in court. All court records are kept by the court itself (usually starting with the county level of government). It is worth your time to look in the indexes to court records (if there are any) to see if your ancestor is mentioned. It's not worth it to go through individual court record books, as you probably won't find anything. Only if the records have been indexed is it worth your time. Then you can follow up on anything you find in the index. Some court records are indexed in just one index. Others use two indexes: one for plaintiffs (the person asking for the court action) and one for defendants (the person defending against the action). As with all of the records I've talked about, always find out about the particular system for the place the records are kept so that you do not miss anything.

Abstract of Will

From: *Berkeley County, W. Va., Will Book 3, p. 376.*

Name of person making will: *Jacob Beller*

Date and place: *31 Mar 1801, Berkeley County, West Virginia*

Date and place probated: *27 Apr 1801, Berkeley County, West Virginia*

Bequests:
1. "Well beloved wife Ann" — "one third part of the income of all my lands and living during her natural life."
2. Son, Jacob — 90 acres of land "where he now dwells."
3. Son, Eli — all the unwilled part of my lands when he arrives at the age of 21. Arrange his schooling and guardianship to age 21.
4. Son, Peter — $8 — his land "I have conveyed to him by deed."
5. Son, Isaac — $10
6. Grandson, Abraham — 50 pounds when he comes of age. Also if Eli dies before age 21 or without heirs then "Abraham, son to my daughter Leah shall have one third of the land divided to my son Eli."
7. Daughter, Lydia — $141
8. Daughter, Naomi Sagatha — $141
9. Daughter, Mary Neal — $141
10. Daughter, Leah Morlatt — $141
11. Daughter, Elizabeth Shaw — $141
12. Daughter, Rachel Harper — $141
13. Grandson, William Shaw — $70 when he comes of age

Name of executors: *John Vanmetre, Nathan Vanmetre, Captain Jacob Vandoran, Nicholas Straye*

Witnesses: *John McMurron, John Booine, William Rush, Jacob Vanmetre*

As I said earlier, these are not records that you will use as often as vital records. But after you have finished with the vital records, it is important to at least check for a will, since if there is one the information will be very helpful. Once you have finished the basics and are starting to fill in background information on your ancestors, you'll find yourself using these local records much more. Each of these records has a possible place in your research, and it's important that you know about all of them for those times when your research comes to a dead end.

A Visit to the Town or County Clerk's Office

This chapter is included for two reasons. The first is to get you ready for a visit to a town or county clerk's office if you will be doing some research there. The second is to give you an idea of what you will find there, even if you can't visit one now.

Before you can go to one of these places to research, you will need to make some plans. The most important plan for you as a student doing research is to have an adult go with you. When I teach a genealogy class we take a field trip to the town clerk's office. If you are working through this book alone, you will need to have someone go with you. I don't know of any town or county clerk's office that will let a student come in to do research alone. This is because the records that are kept there cannot be replaced.

Find out when the office is open. Sometimes these offices are so small that they are only open for a few hours a week. In some cases, the town or county clerk's office is in their own home. You have to check before you go, because the clerk might not be working that day. Some clerks' offices are open on Saturday mornings, but not many of them.

Be sure you have the adult going with you speak with the clerk in advance. The adult should tell the clerk that you are a serious researcher, that you know how to do research, and that you would like to find a time to visit when the office is not too busy. Hopefully, the clerk will then set a date and time.

Rules

The day has arrived. You are going to do your first "real" research. You will be holding in your hands (clean hands, please!) documents that may have been written 200 years ago. You will be holding what, in some cases, is the only copy anywhere of a particular document. This is a big responsibility. Lots of the old deed and will books are falling apart. They are old. They have been handled many, many times over the years. The pages are brittle and pieces come off in your hands very easily. They are difficult to read. Sometimes the ink has faded. Sometimes the ink has bled through from the other side of the page, making the words hard to read. All of this leads to some rules:

1. Make sure you have clean hands.
2. Never use a pen near an old document. Always use a pencil. If you have to point at the words to follow along, use the eraser end of the pencil.
3. Turn pages slowly and carefully.
4. These are usually busy places, so be courteous and quiet.
5. Never, ever have food or drink around records.

In some places the records have become so old and fragile that no one is allowed to use them at all. They have been put on microfilm, and you have to use a special microfilm reader to look at them. If that is the case, someone will show you how to use the reader.

Preparing for Your Visit

Before your visit to the clerk's office to use the records, you should have some idea of what you want to find. If you come to the office and say, "I want some information about the Smith family," you may not get much help. But if you come in and say, "My great-great-grandfather William Smith lived here around 1870. I would like to find birth records of his children, born in the 1880s, his death record around 1925, and whether he owned a farm here," you will probably be able to find some answers.

To be successful, you have to plan ahead. In Chapter 5 we took all the information you had so far and tried to put it in order. We made up a list of what information you still needed to find. To plan for your visit to the clerk's office, start with your list of missing information.

First determine which information on that list will be at this particular clerk's office. If your grandmother was born in Sacramento, California and so were all her brothers and sisters, you won't find her brothers' and sisters' birth certificates in Virginia. Local records are usually kept right where they are. Some of the newer ones are not, but we'll talk about those in the next chapter. For now, we'll say that old vital records (birth, marriage, and death) and deed and will records are kept locally and that is where you have to go to see them. So, the first step is to determine which information that you need is at the clerk's office you plan to visit.

I will use the example of William Smith to show how to get ready for your visit. Look at the unshaded area of the sample note sheet on page 61. Remember, this is just a made-up story, but it has the same kind of information you might be starting with.

Step 1: Write down what you do know.

Step 2: Decide what things in what you know might be in the records. Look first for possible births, marriages, or deaths. Then see about deed records. If there's a death record, then look for a will.

Step 3: Check to see when the records for this office begin.

Step 4: Write down a specific list of records you need to search for.

Notes for visit to clerk's office, Jefferson Cty, W. Va.
Information I already know:

Grandma said her grandfather William Smith moved to Harper's Ferry, W. Va. around 1870 to marry a girl named Sarah. "They lived there and their 6 children were born there — my dad (John), Aunt Katie, Uncle Jim, Aunt Sarah, another girl and a baby who died." He had a big farm and when Grandma was small she used to visit there every summer. Grandma said her grandfather died when she was about 10 (1920?). Her grandmother went to live with Aunt Katie in Ohio and died there a long time later.

Information to look at on this visit

① Marriage – William Smith to Sarah ? around 1870. Get his and her parents, too.	Marr: 18 Jun 1871 William J. Smith Parents: James, Polly Sarah Gibbons Parents: Edward & Ann
② Births	
John 18 Oct 1874	yes 2nd child
Katie	Katherine Elizabeth 1st 6 Jun 1872
Jim	Edward James 4th 3 Feb 1878
Sarah	Sarah Amelia 6th 11 Apr 1885
(girl)	Jane Ann 5th 6 May 1880
baby who died	Baby boy, stillborn 3rd 11 Nov 1876
③ Death – William Smith – around 1920	cannot find
④ Will record – William Smith	
⑤ Deed books – Check index 1870 on	

○		
FG#	What do I need	What to do now
4	Aunt Margaret's first marriage Date, place, full name of spouse	Write to Aunt Margaret and ask for information
8	Wife — need full name (Lizzie) —need birth information —need death certificate (she died "couple of months after William born while visiting parents)	William born in Vermont, 1902. Check death record at Vermont Vital Records. If not found, try for d. cert. where her parents lived (Stockbridge Mass). Use d.cert info to get b. cert.
8	Child — died as infant—born between Joseph (1897) and Henry (1900)	Check b. certs. at Vt. Vital Records for births 1898-99 with that last name
○ 10	Husband — need b. cert. (11 Oct 1886) —need m. cert. ? Dec 1918 —need d. cert. 7 May 1936	Try Vermont Vital Records
12	Child — Rose — need death date (?1967) —need marr. date Sep 1948	Write to Missouri Vital Records (either county or state)
14	Husband — need b.cert. (3 Jul 1890) —need m. cert. (1 Sep 1921) —need d. cert. (18 Nov 1958) Wife — need b. cert. (26 Jun 1891)	Write to Jefferson Cty, W. Va. for records Same
○ 16	Husband — need b. cert. — 1834 —need m. cert. —1852 —need d. cert. —1909 Wife — need b. cert. —1837 —need d. cert. — 1904 Child — have 5 names only out of ?9	Try town records. If not, try Vt. Vital Records Same Check b. records for both areas family lived

Doing Your Research

1. Have your adult helper introduce you. Then show the clerk your detailed list so he or she will know you are prepared.

2. Ask: "I will need to see marriage records for around 1870, birth records for the 1870s and 1880s, death records for around 1920. Are these records indexed and can you show me how to find the books with the records in them?"

3. Use the indexes.

4. Use the records.

5. Copy down everything completely! Copy your information on another piece of paper. On your "Notes" sheet just write yes or no and a quick comment on what you found.

6. After you're finished with vital records, look at what is on your note sheet and decide what to do next.

In the shaded area you can see where I added the information I found on my pretend visit. Remember, these are just notes — the whole record for each of these is on a separate sheet of paper.

I found the marriage and have parents' names. Since there are indexes to vital records here, it's worth a quick check to see if the parents' marriages are recorded.

Sarah's birth in 1885 says seventh child. Check all Smith births between 1880-84 again to see if another child is listed for these parents.

No death record for William. Quickly check will index. If nothing is listed, then maybe William died somewhere else.

7. Go back and finish research for the day doing the deed and will indexes which were not done earlier, the possible marriage of William's and Sarah's parents, and the Smith births for the missing child.

8. If you run into a problem, ask for help. Be polite — you won't get help from the person you interrupt in the middle of doing something else. Be specific. A question like "I found William Smith listed in the index on page 896, but I can't find him on that page. What would you suggest I do?" is more likely to get an answer than "I looked on every page in that stupid book and my ancestor isn't there. Where is he?"

9. Time to go home — don't try to do the whole family in one day!

10. Say thank you. It's still unusual for a town clerk to let a young person in to do research.

Follow-Up At Home

When you get home, take all the information you have found and record it on the family group sheets. Don't put off doing this — in a few days your notes won't make as much sense as they do right now. Once you have recorded your information, make yourself a new list of things you need to find (see the sample on page 62). That way you will always know where you are in your research.

State Records

Sometimes I feel that some of the things I say in a genealogy class I keep saying over and over. The thing I seem to repeat most often is, "It's important that you find out where and what the records are for the area in which you are researching." Each state has different information which you will be able to use for genealogical research. Some states have collected their vital records and made them available to researchers in one place, usually the state capital (like Vermont). Massachusetts has published all of its vital records before 1850 in book form. Some states kept all their yearly tax lists (like Virginia), and these can be used like an annual census record of everyone in the state. Some states have collected and published all of their early records from colonial times (like Pennsylvania). Each state has its own unique system. So you will have to check for the individual state where you will be doing research. What I will go over here is some of the records that you might be lucky enough to find in

your state. This will at least give you an idea of the kinds of records to ask for. Most states have a state archives or state library of some sort, and that is who you should contact first. They will probably be able to send you a pamphlet describing what they own and directing you to other repositories of records in the state.

State Censuses

Many states took their own censuses (counts of all the people in the state) in addition to the national census done every ten years. Since these are state records, they are kept someplace within the state such as the state archives. Most of the really early state censuses (those taken during colonial times before the Revolutionary War) have been printed as books and can be found in genealogical libraries for your state. For later censuses you will have to find out where the records are kept.

Mortality Schedules

Beginning in 1850, when the national censuses (see Chapter 10) were taken, a special section was added that took information on people who died during the year the census was taken. From 1850 to 1880 these censuses, called Mortality Schedules, were collected from the states. The federal government decided to return these schedules to the states in 1919, since they were really copies of local records. Most states chose to take their mortality schedules and place them in their archives. A few states did not, and those schedules are kept at the Daughters of the American Revolution Library in Washington, DC. (We will talk about this in Chapter 11.) These schedules have many death records which may not be available in other places. It is worth it to look for your family names in the schedules for your state.

Vital Records

I mentioned in Chapter 6, when we talked about finding vital records, that in some states copies have been made of all of the vital records and these have been placed in one central place. Most states keep copies of all the modern vital records. Again, you should check to see what's available in your state.

I also mentioned the microfilming project of the Church of Jesus Christ of Latter-day Saints. Many states have placed copies of all the microfilms of these local records for their state in their state archives or library. In Chapter 11 we will talk about using these films through the individual LDS libraries.

One other point about early vital records, particularly the early marriage records, is that many communities have published their early records in book form, so that they can be available everywhere. You will usually find these books wherever your state library collection of genealogical information is kept.

Tax Lists

Some states have on file in their archives their original tax lists back to colonial times. In Virginia, for example, which is a difficult state to research in because of all the lost records, the one very useful set of records available is Personal Property Tax Lists because they go all the way back to early colonial times. Virginia taxed all males over age sixteen, and the yearly lists serve as an annual census. Using these lists, you can trace where people were every single year.

Again, this is a great resource if it exists for your area of research. Tax lists may be for land taxes or personal property taxes. Keep in mind that these may be local records in many areas. It is worth finding out who has these lists for your area and taking a look at them sometime. You won't use them very often, but sometimes they will have the only available piece for your genealogical jigsaw puzzle.

Military Records

We will discuss military records in the next chapter. These are almost all national records which are available through the National Archives. But before we became a country, when we were still colonies, each colony had an army, and those military records stayed with each of the colonial governments as they became state governments. Along with the records of the colonial militias before the Revolutionary War, the original states kept records for their militias that fought in the Revolutionary War. Some of the individual states even gave pensions and land grants to people who had served in the militia. Keep in mind when you get your lines back to Revolutionary War times that if you do not find military records in the National Archives, you might still find them in the state archives for the state your ancestor served in the war.

There is one other type of military record that is not national and therefore is not available at the National Archives. This is the pension records for soldiers who served in the Confederate Army in the Civil War. All of the actual military service records, both Union and Confederate, are held by the National Archives, but people who served in the Confederacy could not get a pension from the federal government later in life if they became ill and could not work. So individual Confederate states decided to give pensions to their former soldiers. These pension records stayed with the individual southern states. If, in researching an ancestor, you find he served in the Confederate Army from Virginia, for example, it would be worth writing to the Virginia State Archives to see if he ever applied for a pension.

Land Grants and Patents

When we discussed deed records in Chapter 7, I said that there was an earlier kind of land record for an original grant of land to the first owner. These are called land grants and patents. For many of the midwestern and western states these are national records, since this land was divided up and given out or sold by various acts of Congress. But for many of the original colonies, these are state records. In colonial times, these were called land patents. These are usually well-kept records and can give you information on when your ancestor arrived in an area and where he came from.

These records are found in the archives of the states, and each had its own system for dividing up the land. Many of these original land grants have been published in book form, giving just the name of the grantee, the size of the grant, and some indication of a grant number. With this information, you are then able to request a copy of the actual grant and its survey. I have a 1750 land grant from the Virginia Northern Neck grants, and I always enjoy reading the closing part about "in the Twenty fourth Year of the Reign of our Sovereign Lord George the Second by the Grace of God of Great Britain France and Ireland King."

Other Records

Some other groups of records tend to find their way into state archives. These include original church records, collections of Bible records, collections of personal papers of famous people, collections of genealogical notes, and collections of maps. Any one of these may have the missing piece to your research — don't pass them by!

10

National Records

This chapter will tell you about some national records. These are records kept by the National Archives in Washington, DC. Some of these old records can be very helpful to you in your genealogical research. We will talk about the three major kinds of national records you might be using. These are census records, military records, and immigration records.

Census Records

When we looked at vital records in Chapter 6, we talked about how much information they have. But we said the problem is that no one kept birth and death records until after the Civil War ended in 1865. Even where the records were kept, they weren't always required until after 1900, so many times we can't find the record we need. Before the 1860s, the situation is

even worse. For most of the country, there are no birth or death records at all. All we can use is will records and hope that all the members of a family will be listed. The one other source that can really help in putting old families together is census records.

When the federal (national) government began counting all the people in the country every ten years, it wasn't because they wanted genealogists to have a good source of research today. The U.S. Constitution says that the House of Representatives has to be set up so that everyone is represented fairly. To do this, someone must count all the people and show where they are so that the areas each representative takes care of have the right number of people. The way the government does this is by counting every person in the country every ten years. This was done for

---

Teachers please note: When I present this information to a class, I always provide a summary handout of census data rather than discussing it in the detail presented here.

the first time in 1790 and has been done every ten years since. Each time the census was taken more questions were asked. The answers to those questions can really help you put together old family groups.

You cannot see census records that are less than seventy-two years old. This protects the privacy of the people listed on them. But even with that rule, you can still see the censuses for 1790, 1800, 1810, 1820, 1830, 1840, 1850, 1860, 1870, 1880, 1890, 1900, and 1910. All of these censuses have been put on microfilm so you look at them by using a microfilm reader. Copies of the censuses are in different places around the country. So you don't have to go to Washington, DC to use them.

The first five censuses (1790-1840) did not give much information at all. They can help you find out where a family was at a certain time and how many people there were in the family. These early censuses always give the name of the head of the family. Then they give the number of males and females in the family by age groups. The age groups get smaller as the censuses go on. In 1790 they gave the number of males sixteen or older and the number under age sixteen. By the 1840 census the question for number of males was in twelve different age groups. In 1820 the census takers asked another question that is helpful for genealogical research. They asked for the number of people in agriculture (farming), commerce (selling things), and manufacturing (making things — like shoemakers, potters, and carpenters). If you find your ancestor in the 1820 census you will be able to find out what he was doing, too.

The important censuses for doing research on your family tree are the ones from the 1850 census on. Starting in 1850, the name of every person in the family was listed so you can use the census to put your families together. Listed below is the information asked for each of the censuses from 1850 to 1910.

1850 Census:
Name of each person in family
Address
Age
Sex
Color
Occupation
Value of any real estate (property or house) you own
Place of birth (only state or country)
Whether person got married this year
Whether person went to school this year
Whether person can read and write

1860 Census:
All the questions from the 1850 Census plus:
Value of personal estate (this is all the things you own besides your house and land)

1870 Census:
All the questions from the 1860 Census plus:
Citizenship of males over twenty-one (this is helpful because there were lots of immigrants arriving at this time, and you can get an idea of how long they have been in the U.S. from this question)
Place of birth of parents
Whether person was born this year

1880 Census:
All the questions from 1870 plus:
Relationship of this person to head of the family

Marital status (single, married, widowed)

Whether person had no job for part of the year

Whether person was sick or disabled for part of the year

1890 Census:

The 1890 Census was very detailed and asked lots of new questions that would be a great help for researchers today. Unfortunately, 99% of the records were destroyed in a fire in 1921. So all that valuable information is lost. Only the census records for 6,160 people were saved. These people lived in Alabama, Washington, DC, or Georgia.

1900 Census (new information for this census is in italics)

Name

Address (street and number this time)

Relationship to head of household

Color and sex

Month and year of birth

Age

Marital status

Number of years married

Number of children born to the mother and number still living

Place of birth

Year of immigration to U.S.

Number of years in U.S.

Whether person is now a U.S. citizen

Occupation and whether unemployed for part of the year

School attendance

Whether person can read and write and speak English

Whether person lives on a farm

Whether person owns a home or rents one

1910 Census

Almost identical to 1900 Census but also asks whether person is a survivor of the Union or Confederate Army or Navy.

Using the Census Records

The census records can be used at the National Archives in Washington, DC and at the eleven regional Archives in Boston, New York, Philadelphia, Atlanta, Chicago, Kansas City, Fort Worth, Denver, Los Angeles, San Francisco, and Seattle. Many state libraries have the census records for their state, so you may not have to go far to see the ones for your state. The Church of Jesus Christ of Latter-day Saints (the Mormons) have genealogical libraries throughout the country. If you have one near you, you can rent census microfilms from their main library in Salt Lake City, UT, and use them at their library in your area.

Census records are done by state, so first you need to know which state your ancestors lived in. A private company has made indexes for all the states for all censuses up to 1850 and the 1860 census is being done. The National Archives has a partial index to the 1880 Census and the 1910 Census and a complete index to the 1900 Census. You will have to ask someone to teach you how to use these indexes since the 1880, 1900, and 1910 indexes are on microfilm and use a tricky system called a Soundex. The older census indexes are in books and are just like the indexes you are used to using.

The censuses have lots of mistakes in them. We mentioned earlier that the records are not always accurate. The censuses are very inaccurate. The worst part is people's names. The census takers wrote down what they thought they heard, and sometimes their spelling wasn't too great. Sometimes it wasn't their fault — a person named Mary Anne might be listed as Mary Anne in 1860 and by 1870 her family just called her "Mary" and she is listed that way. Sometimes people gave their nicknames instead of their given names. So using the census records is really like putting together a jigsaw puzzle!

Some of the census takers were also very lazy. Some didn't bother asking all the questions or filling in all the answers very well. Some used ink that has faded so badly that you can't read the writing at all. And the handwriting was often terrible. You may need to use a magnifying glass to decode the writing on the page. But you will find it so much fun that the hardest part will be looking for your own family without stopping to look at everyone else on the page.

Military Records

The National Archives has all the military service and pension records that exist for all the wars before World War I. For the early wars such as the Revolutionary War and the War of 1812 there are very few records left, but they are worth looking at when you get your family tree to that point. Most of the records you will find are Muster Rolls and Pay Rolls. On the next page is a copy of some War of 1812 service records for Ephraim Beller, my husband's great-great-grandfather. As you can see, it doesn't provide very much information. But if you were looking for an unusual name and went to the general index to

records from the War of 1812, the record could tell you quite a bit. You would learn that Ephraim was a corporal, that from August 23, 1814 to September 19, 1814 he was at a camp near Baltimore, and that his home was in Shepherdstown, Virginia, eighty miles from Baltimore. With that information you would have a state and town so you could begin looking for information there. You could also look up history books on the War of 1812 and see if anything interesting happened while your ancestor was there.

The really useful military records are the pension records. To receive a pension (money from the government for someone who served in a war and now cannot work for himself), the soldier or his widow (for a widow's pension) had to prove his military service. He also had to give some information about himself. If a widow applied to receive her husband's pension, she had to show where they were married and give information on their children. Some of these pension applications can give you all sorts of answers. I was researching a Revolutionary War soldier and could not find any service records for him. (Many records have been lost in fires, so do not be surprised if you can't find them.) I then went to the pension records and found that he had applied for and received a pension. In his pension application I found out that he had fought in the Battle of Fort Washington and was taken prisoner. If a pension record exists, it is definitely worth looking at. So don't give up if you don't find a military service record. Keep looking!

Most of the military service records themselves are available only at the National Archives in Washington, DC. Most

| B | 57
(Lieut. Col. Mason.)
(Lieut. Col. Minor.) | Va.
Militia. | B | 57
(Lieut. Col. Mason.)
(Lieut. Col. Minor.) | Va.
Militia. |

Ephraim Beller

Appears with the rank of _Cpl_ on a

Muster Roll

of a Company of Light Infantry Volunteers (who were accepted and received into service for 60 days unless sooner discharged) commanded by Captain Van Bennett, now attached to the 57 Reg't Virginia Militia,

(War of 1812,)

for _Aug 23_, 1814, when took up the line of march, to _Sept 19_, 1814.

Roll dated _Camp near Baltimore_, _Sept 18_, 1814.

Date of commission, ..., 181 .

Commencement of service, _Aug 24_, 1814.

Expiration of service or } _Sept 18_, 1814.
of this muster,

Distance from Baltimore to Shepherdstown, their respective homes, after } _75 miles_
being discharged,

Present or absent, _Present_

REMARK: Each man belonging to this Co. is allowed 5 days for travelling from Baltimore to Shepherdstown, the distance computed to be 80 miles.

Remarks and alterations since our services were

accepted : ....
....
....
....
....

Ephraim Beller

Appears with the rank of _1 Cpl_ on a

Pay Roll

of a Company of Light Infantry commanded by Capt. Van Bennett, attached to the 57 Reg't Virginia Militia, in service at Baltimore,

(War of 1812,)

for _Aug 24 to Sept 23_, 1814.

Roll dated ....

.... _Sept 23_, 1814.

Commencement of service } _Aug 24_, 1814.
or of this settlement,

Expiration of service or } _Sept 23_, 1814.
of this settlement,

Term of service charged, ... _1_ months, _1_ days.

Pay per month, ... _10_ dollars, ... cents.

Amount of pay, ... _10_ dollars, _24_ cents.

Remarks : ....
....
....
....
....
....
....
....

of the indexes and the entire set of pension records for the Revolutionary War are on microfilm, so you can see those at the Regional Archives. There is a book called the *Index of Revolutionary War Pension Applications in the National Archives*, published by the National Genealogical Society. This is an index to all the pension records and bounty land grants for Revolutionary War veterans. Most libraries with even a medium-sized genealogy collection will have a copy. If you find your ancestor, you can write to the National Archives and they will make you a copy of the main parts of the pension file for your ancestor. There is a small charge for this, based on how many pages they have to copy.

Immigration Records

The immigration records kept at the National Archives are mostly passenger lists for ships arriving in the U.S. from 1819 on. These are very difficult to use because they are arranged by "Port of Entry" — the city where the ship arrived. These are not a good source for your research. You could spend forever and not find your ancestor unless you know exactly when they came and where they arrived. But don't despair — a major project was begun seven years ago to try to index all these records. Several books have been published of the names indexed. These volumes should be available at any library with a good genealogy collection. (We'll be talking about libraries in the next chapter.)

P. William Filby. *Passenger and Immigration Lists Index*. Detroit: Gale Research Company, 1981 and on (multivolume, by 1986, 1,500,000 names).

Dr. Ira A. Glazier and Dr. Michael H. Tepper. *The Famine Immigrants: List of Irish Immigrants Arriving at the Port of New York, 1846-1851*. Baltimore: Genealogical Publishing Company, 1983-86 (7 volumes, 560,000 names).

Dr. Michael H. Tepper. *Passenger Arrivals at the Port of Philadelphia 1800-1819*. Baltimore: Genealogical Publishing Company, 1985 (40,000 names).

Gary J. Zimmerman and M. Wolfert. *German Immigrants: List of Passengers bound from Bremen to New York 1847-1854, 1855-1862*. Baltimore: Genealogical Publishing Company, 1985, 1986 (70,000 names).

Dr. Ira A. Glazier and P. William Filby. *Germans to America 1850-1855* (in progress — 700,000 names).

This list of books gives me a chance to introduce you to the Beller Law for Genealogy: NEVER pass up a chance to look at an index to anything. You can sometimes find great pieces of information by just browsing through genealogical materials. Any set of books with 1,500,000 names is always worth looking at. I once passed up the chance to look at an index to the 1870 Mortality Schedules for West Virginia. This index had just arrived at my local library in Virginia, and I told the librarian that since I had looked at all the county vital records already, there would be no point in looking at this index. One day the librarian was looking for something else in the index. He happened to come across a death record for someone I had been looking for for years. I had missed the person when I searched the vital records at the county clerk's office.

The librarian called me immediately with the information. I have ALWAYS looked at any index I can since then.

With this chapter we finish our discussion of "official records." We began with records kept locally, in your town or county, and worked up through state records, and finally to national records.

These last chapters have covered all the kinds of records you need to know about as your family tree goes further back and becomes harder to research. There is yet another kind of material we need to discuss — that available in libraries and historical societies. These sources are discussed in the next chapter.

Other Records:
Libraries and Historical Societies

In the last five chapters we have looked at those records known as "official records." These records are called primary sources. They are the actual documents of events that happened in the past. In this chapter we will learn about another kind of material you can use in your research.

When someone looks at primary sources and then writes a history from them, that book is a secondary source. Secondary sources are written based on research in primary sources. If you look up all the information in vital records, land records, will records, census records, and military records about your great-great-grandfather who fought in the Civil War, you are using primary sources. If you then write a biography of your great-great-grandfather using the information you found in your research, that biography will be a secondary source.

Secondary sources are usually books or magazine articles. These sources can be found in libraries or historical society collections. Does that mean you can run out to your local library and do all your research there? Unfortunately, no. The kinds of books written on genealogy are usually very expensive ones. That means that most local libraries do not have the money to buy them. Instead, some libraries in an area build up a genealogy collection to be used by people in the surrounding area. Sometimes this is a regional library or a county library. It may be a state library or a state historical society, or a state university may have such a collection. So you may have to do some looking to find the best collection in your area.

For example, in Vermont where I live, there is a small collection at the Fletcher Free Library in Burlington (Vermont's largest city). There is a very large collection at the University of Vermont's library. There is also a collection of archival materials (I'll explain these shortly) and books at the Vermont Historical Society in Montpelier (the state capital). There is a collection of documentary genealogical materials (such as censuses) in the Law

Library section of the Vermont State Library, also in Montpelier. In Virginia, where I lived before moving to Vermont, there is usually a "Virginiana" Room in one of the libraries in each county. But the two major collections are at the Virginia State Library in Richmond (the capital) and at the University of Virginia Library in Charlottesville. Each state and each area will have its own system, so check to find out which is best for your research.

Kinds of Materials to Be Found

Once you find a genealogical collection near enough to visit, what should you find there? The one thing that your library should have plenty of is books. Most genealogical collections have lots of county and local histories for their area. The histories of an area can have a great deal of information. They will tell about the first settlers to reach the area, as well as the early churches, newspapers, and businesses. In each of these histories you will find names from your town, and many times these will be names you can use.

Besides local histories, your genealogical collection will have lots of books of genealogies of people from your area. People who do research usually try to publish it at some time. Since a lot of their research is done at the genealogical collection in their area, they usually give that library a copy of their research. If you happen to be part of one of the lines in a published genealogy, all the research on that line is done for you. But you should never just copy it and assume that it is perfectly correct. You should still check back on the sources for the information yourself. The nice thing about finding a published genealogy is that then you know exactly where to look to find these sources.

Most local histories have some sort of a biographical dictionary of early residents of the area. This is a listing of short biographies of people in the area. These can be a starting place for more research. However, these listings are usually not very accurate and don't give very detailed information.

Genealogical collections usually include any primary records from the area that have been put into published form. Many towns and counties have published their early marriage records, for example. That way they can be used in libraries all over the country. Members of historical societies sometimes go through and copy down all the cemetery gravestone inscriptions and publish those. Sometimes people index old newspapers and publish the indexes. In some places the old deed and will books have been abstracted and any name mentioned in them is published in a book.

Archival Material

The other kind of primary material you might find is archival or manuscript material. This is original material that is donated to a library or historical society to be preserved. Most of this deals with famous people whose "papers" are donated. Their papers can include just about anything — old letters, diaries, Bible records, record books about their farms, etc. The other kind of archival material might be old church records, records of social groups or clubs, or maps or copies of old posters — any original material of historical importance. This type of material can be a good source for information you can't find anywhere else.

I have one story for you about archival material. Thomas Jefferson, the author of the Declaration of Independence and the third President of the United States, kept record books (he called them his farm books) about everyone who visited him at his home, Monticello, near Charlottesville, Virginia. When he died his will stated that all of his papers were to go to the new University of Virginia which he had founded. Over the years, because Jefferson was so important, his farm books were printed and indexed. Jefferson wrote down all of the local events in the Charlottesville area, and many people have been able to find information on their ancestors in his farm books that is not in any of the public records. These records are used all the time by historians. Remember, when you are doing genealogical research, you are a historian, too!

Old Newspapers

Another great source of information kept in genealogical libraries is old newspapers. Newspapers (especially local ones) have all kinds of interesting information in them. Old newspapers are very different from our newspapers today. They are also a lot of fun to read. They are not at all like the other sources we use in doing genealogical research. We always look first for the official documentary records that tell us when a person lived and where. Local histories can give us some idea of what a place was like when our ancestors lived there. But even local histories are written as "history." Because of that, they only talk about the "important" things that happened. Newspapers are different. They give us a day-by-day or week-by-week look at what it really was like to be living in a certain place at a certain time. Newspapers have all of the gossip and trivia of our ancestors' lives — the things that are not important enough to be a part of the history books. When you are doing research, the important thing you will find about using newspapers is that they write about the "ordinary" people, not just the "important" people.

Old newspapers can give you many different kinds of information:

Professional notices: In the times before the telephone and yellow pages, the only way people like lawyers, doctors, dentists, insurance agents, and land agents could announce their business was in newspapers.

Business advertisements: Let's say when you use the deed record you find that your ancestor owned a store in town. You'll want to look at the old newspapers so you can see the ads he placed for his business. They weren't big full-page ads like we see in the newspapers today. These were small ads and many of them make funny reading today.

Public notices: Remember, back before telephones and television, anything you wanted to announce you had to put in the newspaper. So you will find overdue tax lists, lists of people who need to pick up their mail at the post office, notices of church and club meetings, notices for meetings of the volunteer firemen and the militia, and many other kinds of lists.

Public sales: These notices are still in our papers today. They announce sales of estates (wills) or court ordered sales of property. I once found a public sale for someone who had "disappeared" from the official records in the area. Then I found the announcement of the public sale of their personal property (property that is not land or house) since they were moving to Indiana. That gave me the clue I needed to look for them somewhere else.

Personal ads: These include ads for lost and found items, places for rent or sale, legal notices, and help wanted ads. Some of these have information you won't find anywhere else. I once had a client who couldn't figure out her ancestor's occupation. He was listed in the census as a merchant, but when she looked at deed records she couldn't find a store that he owned. I later found him for her while I was looking at old newspapers for something else. He was a merchant. He bought and sold slaves.

News articles: In old newspapers there are very few news articles. Some of the ones there are well worth reading. They give information which will make your ancestors seem very real. One woman's name appeared in a West Virginia newspaper for sending the editor a radish "which measures two and a half feet in circumference, and weighs eleven and a half pounds." (*Spirit of Jefferson*, 24 December 1850).

Marriage notices and obituaries: These are extremely helpful in places where the public records are missing.

Church Records

There is one other kind of record that doesn't fit into any other category. That is church records. Churches keep records of some of the same events that vital records cover — births, marriages, and deaths. In cases where the vital records are missing, the churches may have the only records of these events. In Greene County, Missouri, for example, many of the vital records were lost in a fire. But I have been able to get the information I need on ancestors living there by using church records and old newspapers. So it is important to remember that these exist.

The problem with using church records is availability. Some denominations (like the Presbyterians) have microfilms of all their old records available, and you can borrow them easily through interlibrary loan. Other denominations (like the Methodists and Catholics) keep their records in the local churches. If that is the case, it is up to the pastor of the local church to decide whether to let you use the records, or even to look up the answers for you if you are not allowed to use the records. If copies have been made of church records, however, they are usually put into genealogical collections.

Most of the genealogical collections you will use will have some of each of these kinds of materials. But there are four very special genealogical collections that you should also know about and plan to visit someday.

Major Genealogical Collections

As genealogy has become more popular, many public libraries and university libraries have developed collections of genealogical material. Historical societies have also strengthened their genealogical collections. But there are four genealogical collections that are very special. The first (and the largest in the world) is the

Genealogical Library in Salt Lake City, Utah. The Church of Jesus Christ of Latter-day Saints has spent over thirty years going to all parts of the U.S. and several other countries making microfilm copies of all the old records they can find. Their members have indexed these records. They have the most complete index to birth, marriage, and death records in the world, and it gets bigger with every passing week. Along with this index they have a fantastic collection of published family genealogies and other secondary genealogical sources. This is the place that every genealogist (including me!) hopes to visit someday. What is great is that there are branches of the library throughout the United States where you can use this huge index and pay to rent some of the material from Utah. No other library in the world comes close to matching this fantastic source of information for your research.

The remaining three libraries are in the Washington, DC area. The first is the Library of Congress, which is the largest library in the United States. The Library of Congress has the best collection of local histories and old newspapers in existence. They also have all the basic genealogical sources that most libraries cannot afford to buy. The only problem with this collection is that it can only be used in the Library of Congress itself. That means that you will need to visit and give yourself lots of time to learn how to use it.

The third collection is the Daughters of the American Revolution (D.A.R.) Library, also in Washington, DC. The D.A.R. is made up of women who can prove that they have an ancestor who fought in the Revolutionary War as a patriot. The D.A.R. Library has a fantastic collection of military records and very early records for the first years after the Revolutionary War. These records and books are collected so that people can try to prove their lineage to a Revolutionary patriot. Many of the women who become members of the D.A.R. give copies of their research to the Library, so it also has an excellent collection of published genealogies. The individual D.A.R. chapters around the U.S. also work very hard to find as many sources of information as they can to send to the library. These chapters are best known for collecting old Bible records and copying the tombstones in cemeteries (especially small family graveyards with only a few stones). They send copies of this information to D.A.R. headquarters in Washington, DC so it can be used by everyone who comes to the library. Their dedication to this work has helped them build a collection of materials different from those found in any other collection.

The fourth collection is the library of the National Genealogical Society in Alexandria, Virginia. This library is not a very big one, but it is a lending library. Members of the National Genealogical Society can pay to borrow books in their collection. So if you can't get to any other collection, you might want to keep this one in mind.

Many of these places you will not be able to do research in. But it is important to know that they are there. Maybe you can get an adult interested enough to be your assistant and research at some of these places for you.

Taking a Field Trip:
Continuing the Search

My genealogy students always take a field trip for our twelfth class. We travel to our state capital, Montpelier, to spend a morning at the Vital Records Division and an afternoon at the library of the Vermont Historical Society. Vital Records gives us a chance to practice what we've learned. The library gives us an opportunity to handle some of the printed material mentioned in earlier classes, and to enjoy the experience of handling archival material for the first time. Upon our return, we discuss where each student can go from there to add to his research.

Since I cannot take you on a field trip, I will talk about doing so (an extension of what we did in Chapter 8). I also want to review what we discussed earlier in terms of the order in which you do research. Finally, I want to cover some other sources of information that I haven't mentioned. I'll also share with you my "pep talk" as a final reminder of why you've spent these weeks assembling your own genealogy jigsaw puzzle.

Field Trips

If you decide to take a field trip, be prepared in advance. Evaluate the research you have already done, and decide what research can be done on this visit. It's a good idea to obtain ahead of time a copy of the rules of the place or places you will visit. Go over them thoroughly. Remember that most of these places do not allow students as researchers, so your behavior is very important.

Most organizations have a summary information sheet with a list of rules. A copy of this sheet for Vermont Vital Records follows on the next pages. Some organizations require more than just signing in. Some ask you to fill out an actual application form (the Virginia State Archives has this requirement, as does the National Archives in Washington). Some will not allow you to bring in a briefcase, or may require you to use only pencils. The purpose of these rules is to protect the records.

Determine which research facility in

WELCOME TO VERMONT VITAL RECORDS

FACILITIES: You may park in any of the state parking lots. Rest rooms are on the third floor of this building. (Enter through green door next to ours and take elevator or stairs to 3). Cafeterias are located in the building in front of this one and in the state capitol building.

HOURS: We are open Monday through Friday (except state holidays) from 8 to 12 and from 1 to 4. We will not be responsible for personal belongings left here during lunch hour or at any other time. Children are allowed only if properly managed and quiet.

ACCOMODATIONS: We can accommodate no more than ten persons comfortably at any one time. We suggest that others return at another time or use the microfilm copies upstairs. You may copy information by hand from the cards (preferably with pencil). Scrap paper is available.

HOLDINGS: We have Vermont birth, death and marriage records (state-wide) from 1760 through 1954. These are inter-filed in alphabetical and chronological order under the surname within each of the four year-groups which are quite plainly marked, numbered and color-tagged:

| 1760-1870 | 1870-1908 | 1909-1941 | 1942-1954 |
| (white) | (green) | (orange) | |

Within each drawer the cards are also color-coded. White cards are births, blue cards are deaths, orange cards are cemetery records, yellow cards are marriages. Marriage records are cross-indexed under both the groom and the bride. Some birth and death records have no given names and are filed before any other cards directly after the surname header. Events before 1857 were recorded only voluntarily, so may not be here. Page numbers on upper right-hand corners mean nothing.

RULES:

1. Please register in our guest book once each day. You do not need to sign out when you leave.

2. Leave your briefcases and other unnecessary books, etc. on the floor or platform near the white post. Use only as much table space as you need.

3. Observe signs posted around the room.

(OVER)

4. Remove only <u>one</u> drawer at a time. Replace it before removing another.

5. Handle cards carefully - they are extremely brittle from age.

6. Always work at the table if possible. Aisle space is limited.

7. Try to work quietly. It is important to everyone that the noise level be kept to a minimum.

8. Please notify staff if you find a card out of order.

9. Please alert staff if you observe anyone removing cards from drawers.

10. Make sure drawer is returned to its proper place. They are color-tagged and numbered for your convenience.

11. Do not hesitate to ask for assistance if cards are too tight in the drawer you are using. We will be most happy to help you.

12. Please put your drawer away before leaving.

13. Help yourself to maps and literature on the registration table.

WARNING:

DO NOT RAISE THE CARDS UP OUT OF THEIR POSITION IN THE DRAWER! DO NOT TAKE CARDS OUT OF THE DRAWERS FOR ANY REASON! ONLY STAFF MEMBERS ARE ALLOWED TO REMOVE THE CARDS.

DO NOT LEAVE CARDS STICKING UP CROOKEDLY IN THE DRAWER. MAKE SURE ALL CARDS ARE DOWN FLUSH BEFORE PUTTING DRAWER AWAY.

DO NOT ATTEMPT TO REMOVE THE DRAWERS IN THE 1942-1954 GROUP. STAFF MEMBERS WILL REMOVE A SMALL SECTION FOR YOU.

NEVER, NEVER MARK ON THE CARDS!

Thank You For Your Cooperation In Our Effort To Maintain And Preserve These Very Important Public Records For Future Generations.

your area is your best source. Some areas have a wealth of choices available. For example, when I taught an advanced genealogy course for adults in Fairfax County, Virginia, we went to the Virginiana Room at the main Fairfax County library, since it was close to us. But when the course was completed, I always offered an unofficial field trip to the Virginia State Archives and Library and the Virginia Historical Society Library in Richmond, 100 miles away. The instructors for the basic genealogy courses chose from the National Archives, the Library of Congress, the D.A.R. Library, and the National Genealogical Society Library for their field trips. Not everyone doing research has this kind of selection, but I'm sure you can find useful sources in your community.

Continuing Your Research

You've decided that genealogy is fun, that finding your "story" is something you want to continue. So now what do you do?

Most of your genealogical research comes from a limited number of records. Those records are your starting point. They are the ones we've discussed in this book. As a general rule, in doing genealogical research, you start with your own family records, use vital records next, and then move on to deed and will records. Census and military records are your next large category. Along the way, you fill in from state records and secondary sources such as local histories, published genealogies, and old newspapers. You might visit old cemeteries that haven't been cataloged yet.

Another important source is other researchers. Over the years, the people I've met have provided much information and encouragement in my own research. You meet people at the places you do research, and by joining local historical and genealogical societies. Many of these organizations put out letters or journals that allow you to place "Queries." These are small ads where you give the name of the person you are researching so that other people can help you find information. There is one journal that has 48,000 genealogists as subscribers. It is called the *Genealogical Helper* (published six times a year, $17 for an annual subscription, by The Everton Publishers, Inc., P.O. Box 368, Logan, UT 84321). It includes a few articles about researching and reviews of new genealogy books, but it is most useful as a means for people to advertise for needed genealogical information. An ad I placed several years ago prompted eighteen letters, and it was for a very uncommon name. Your local library may subscribe to this if it has a genealogical collection. You will find it to be a great place to find out who else is researching your family lines. It also will put you in touch with all of the family newsletters and associations. Once a year, it lists all of the genealogical libraries and organizations for each state — information you will need.

When I say that people are a great source, I am including all of the unofficial ways in which you can find genealogical information. Much of your success in finding pieces to your family jigsaw puzzle will depend on luck. Once when I was teaching a course, a woman taking it had to miss a class as she was going to Colonial Williamsburg, Virginia for a vacation. As she was touring the buildings, she came upon a plaque that included a last name she was researching. She asked about it and, with incredible luck, managed to fill in an entire missing line of her genealogy. Her story shows how important it is always to be on the lookout for new information and not to be afraid to ask questions. There are all sorts of unusual places out there where you might find information: schools people attended may have their records, organizations people joined may have records, places people worked or retirement organizations they belonged to - any source you can think of. I was once trying to fill in a fairly recent family group sheet. The family member I spoke with knew only that her uncle, Willis, had moved somewhere down south after he retired, and no one had ever heard from him afterwards. He had worked for a railroad. That piece of information, over the course of two years, led to receiving a copy of his pension papers and death record from the Railroad Retirement Board in Chicago. He had died in Charlotte, North Carolina, and no one in the family had ever known.

I also have pictures of a plaque located in the West Virginia Press Association Hall of Fame in Morgantown, West Virginia, and dedicated to James W. Beller, the founder of the *Spirit of Jefferson* newspapers and the hero of my "coffin" story in Chapter 1. The fact that the plaque was there came from a conversation with an elderly resident of Charles Town, West Virginia, who was reminiscing about the two elderly unmarried daughters who lived next door to her when she was a child. All this leads to Beller's Second Law of Genealogy: Never be afraid to ask questions — every once in a while the information you get will be fantastic!

Putting the Jigsaw Puzzle Together

If you have followed along with the homework in this book, you are well on your way to having five generations of your genealogy on your group sheets. You have probably already discovered some dead ends — people for whom the jigsaw puzzle pieces may never be found. That is discouraging, and sometimes it's frustrating to realize that some of these will never be complete. You've also found though, some lines that want to just run back on their own. At Vital Records in Montpelier, one of my students came upon a string of marriages that brought her line two generations past her five generation chart. Imagine her excitement!

Genealogy has its ups and downs. If you think that you are going to find everything and wrap up all your research in six months or a year, then this is not the hobby for you. I have some lines for which I have not been able to find anything for years. But I don't give up — I just get stubborn and more determined. In the meantime, I work on other lines, and come back to the ones I'm stuck on only when something new is published for that area.

Genealogy is not for everybody. There is a lot of detailed work involved, and some of the research gets boring after a while. However, completing the first five generations and preserving family stories for that time period is a reasonable goal for anyone to achieve. Beyond that, the search for more records is for those who truly have the desire to make it a lifelong hobby. Whatever you do, do not throw out any of the research you have done while working through this book. What you have done is history. Put it aside if you want to. Then, twenty or thirty years from now, when the urge to find out more comes back (and it will!), you will have a head start and will have preserved some stories of people who may be long dead by then. For those of you who want to go on now, I've included a list of places where you can get supplies and forms in the appendix. I've also included a bibliography of other books with which to continue your research.

For everyone, whether you keep researching now or come back to it later, remember that you are unique and the collection of stories in your history is special to you. Good luck in putting together your family jigsaw puzzle, and most of all, have fun with it!

Appendices

Family Group Sheet Number: _____

Husband: _____

	Date	Place	Source
Birth:			
Marriage:			
Death:			
Occupation:		Military Service:	
Church:		Other Marriages:	
Father:		Mother:	

Wife: _____

	Date	Place	Source
Birth:			
Marriage:			
Death:			
Occupation:			
Church:		Other Marriages:	
Father:		Mother:	

Children (Start with oldest):

Name	Birth	Marriage	Spouse	Death

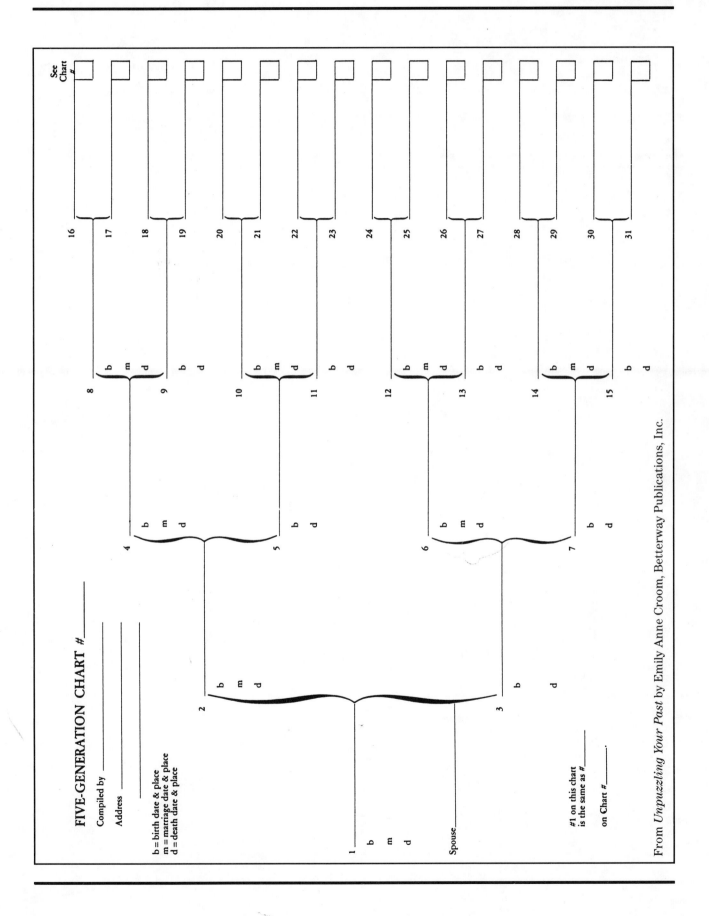

FIVE-GENERATION CHART #

Compiled by _____

Address _____

b = birth date & place
m = marriage date & place
d = death date & place

#1 on this chart
is the same as #_____

on Chart #_____.

From *Unpuzzling Your Past* by Emily Anne Croom, Betterway Publications, Inc.

Abstract of Deed

County: Deed Book: Page:

Name of Grantor:

Name of Grantee:

Description of Property:

Amount Paid:

Witnesses:

Legal Description of Property (if names included):

Abstract of Will

Name of person making will:

Date and place:

Date and place probated:

Bequests:

Name of executors:

Witnesses:

1790 CENSUS

Township or Local Community _____

Enumerator _____ Date Census Taken _____

_____ County _____ State _____

Enumerator District # _____

Page	Name of Head of Family	Free White Males 16 years & upwards including heads of families	Free White Males under 16 years	Free White Females including heads of families	All Other Free Persons	Slaves	Dwellings / Other information

From *Unpuzzling Your Past* by Emily Anne Croom, Betterway Publications, Inc.

1800 or 1810 CENSUS

Local Community _____ County _____ State _____

Enumerator _____ Date Census Taken _____ Enumerator District # _____ Supervisor District # _____

Written Page No.	Printed Page No.	Name of Head of Family	Free White Males						Free White Females						All other free persons except Indians not taxed	Slaves
			under 10	of 10 & under 16	of 16 & under 26	of 26 & under 45	of 45 & up		under 10	of 10 & under 16	of 16 & under 26	of 26 & under 45	of 45 & up			
					including heads of families						including heads of families					

From *Unpuzzling Your Past* by Emily Anne Croom, Betterway Publications, Inc.

Local Community _____

Enumerator _____

1820 CENSUS

County _____ State _____

Date Census Taken _____ Enumerator District # _____

Supervisor District # _____

Written Page No.	Printed Page No.	Name of Head of Family	Free White Males						Free White Females					Foreigners Not Naturalized	Persons engaged in Agriculture	Persons engaged in Commerce	Persons engaged in Manufacture	Free Colored Persons								All other persons	Slaves
					including heads of families					including heads of families								Males				Females					
			to 10	10 to 16	*16 to 18	16 to 26	26 to 45	45 & up	to 10	10 to 16	16 to 26	26 to 45	45 & up					to 14	14 to 26	26 to 45	45 & up	to 14	14 to 26	26 to 45	45 & up		

* Those males between 16 & 18 will all be repeated in the column of those between 16 and 26.

From *Unpuzzling Your Past* by Emily Anne Croom, Betterway Publications, Inc.

1830 or 1840 CENSUS Part 1

Local Community _____

Enumerator _____

State _____

County _____

Date Census Taken _____

Enumerator District # _____

Supervisor District # _____

Written Page No.	Printed Page No.	Name of Head of Family	Free White Persons (including heads of families)																								
			Males													Females											
			under 5	5-10	10-15	15-20	20-30	30-40	40-50	50-60	60-70	70-80	80-90	90-100	100& over	under 5	5-10	10-15	15-20	20-30	30-40	40-50	50-60	60-70	70-80	80-90	90-100	100& over

From *Unpuzzling Your Past* by Emily Anne Croom, Betterway Publications, Inc.

1830 CENSUS   Part 2

Local Community _____

Enumerator _____

State _____

County _____   Date Census Taken _____

Enumerator District # _____

Supervisor District # _____

Written Page No.	Printed Page No.	Name of Head of Family (from previous page)	Slaves — Males under 10	10–24	24–36	36–55	55–100	100 & up	Slaves — Females under 10	10–24	24–36	36–55	55–100	100 & up	Free Colored Persons — Males under 10	10–24	24–36	36–55	55–100	100 & up	Free Colored Persons — Females under 10	10–24	24–36	36–55	55–100	100 & up	TOTAL	White Persons included in the foregoing who are deaf & dumb under 14	deaf & dumb 14–25	deaf & dumb 25 & up	blind	foreigners not naturalized	Slaves & Colored Persons included in the foregoing who are deaf & dumb under 14	deaf & dumb 14–25	deaf & dumb 25 & up	blind

From *Unpuzzling Your Past* by Emily Anne Croom, Betterway Publications, Inc.

1840 CENSUS   Part 2

Local Community ———————————
Enumerator ———————————
State ———————————
County ———————————
Date Census Taken ———————————
Enumerator District # ———————
Supervisor District # ———————

Written Page No.	Printed Page No.	Name of Head of Family (Previous Page)	Free Colored Persons — Males						Free Colored Persons — Females						Slaves — Males						Slaves — Females						T O T A L	Number of Persons employed in each family in — Mining	Agriculture	Commerce	Manufacturing & Trades	Ocean Navigation	Canal, Lake, River Navigat'n	Learned Prof'ns & Engineers	Revolutionary or Military Service Pensioners in the foregoing — Name	Age
			under 10	10–24	24–36	36–55	55–100	100 & up	under 10	10–24	24–36	36–55	55–100	100 & up	under 10	10–24	24–36	36–55	55–100	100 & up	under 10	10–24	24–36	36–55	55–100	100 & up										

From *Unpuzzling Your Past* by Emily Anne Croom, Betterway Publications, Inc.

1850 CENSUS

Post Office or
Local Community _____

State _____

Enumerator District # _____

Supervisor District # _____

County _____

Enumerator _____

Date Census Taken _____

Written Page No.	Printed Page No.	Dwelling in order of visitation	Family Number in order of visitation	Name of every person whose usual place of abode on 1 June 1850 was with this family	Description			Profession, Occupation, or Trade of each Male over 15	Value of of Real Estate Owned	Place of Birth naming state, territory, or country	Married within the year	In School within the year	Persons over 20 unable to read & write	If deaf & dumb, blind, insane, idiot, pauper or convict
					Age	Sex	Color							
		1	2	3	4	5	6	7	8	9	10	11	12	13

From *Unpuzzling Your Past* by Emily Anne Croom, Betterway Publications, Inc.

1860 CENSUS

Post Office or
Local Community _____ State _____

Enumerator _____ County _____ Enumerator District # _____

Date Census Taken _____ Supervisor District # _____

Written Page No.	Printed Page No.	Dwelling Number	Family Number	Name of every person whose usual place of abode on 1 June 1860 was with this family	Description			Profession, Occupation, or Trade of each person over 15	Value of Real Estate Owned	Value of Personal Estate Owned	Place of Birth naming state, territory or country	Married within the year	In school within the year	Persons over 20 unable to read & write	Deaf & dumb, blind, insane, idiotic, pauper, or convict
					Age	Sex	Color								
		1	2	3	4	5	6	7	8	9	10	11	12	13	14

From *Unpuzzling Your Past* by Emily Anne Croom, Betterway Publications, Inc.

1870 CENSUS

Local Community _____

Enumerator _____

State _____

County _____

Date Census Taken _____

Enumerator District # _____

Supervisor District # _____

Written Page No.	Printed Page No.	Dwelling No. 1	Family No. 2	Name of every person whose place of abode on 1 June 1870 was in this family 3	Description — Age 4	Sex 5	Color 6	Profession, Occupation, or Trade 7	Value of — Real Estate Owned 8	Personal Estate Owned 9	Place of Birth 10	Parents — Father Foreign-born 11	Mother Foreign-born 12	Month born within the year 13	Month married within the year 14	In school within the year 15	Cannot read 16	Cannot write 17	Deaf & dumb, blind, insane or idiotic 18	Males eligible to vote 19	Males not eligible to vote 20

From *Unpuzzling Your Past* by Emily Anne Croom, Betterway Publications, Inc.

1880 CENSUS

Local Community _____

Enumerator _____

County _____   State _____

Date Census Taken _____   Supervisor District # _____

Enumerator District # _____

Written Page No.	Printed Page No.	Street Name	House Number	Dwelling Number (1)	Family Number (2)	Name of every person whose place of abode on 1 June 1880 was in this family (3)	Description			Month born if during census year (7)	Relationship to head of this household (8)	Single (9)	Married (10)	Widowed / Divorced (11)	Married during year (12)	Profession, Occupation or Trade (13)	Months unemployed this year (14)	Currently ill? If so, specify. (15)	Health					School this year (21)	Cannot read (22)	Cannot write (23)	Birthplace (24)	Birthplace of Father (25)	Birthplace of Mother (26)
							Color (4)	Sex (5)	Age (6)										Blind (16)	Deaf & dumb (17)	Idiotic (18)	Insane (19)	Disabled (20)						

From *Unpuzzling Your Past* by Emily Anne Croom, Betterway Publications, Inc.

1900 CENSUS

Local Community _____
Ward _____
Enumerator _____

State _____
Supervisor District # _____
Enumeration District # _____

County _____
Date Census Taken _____

Written Page No.	Printed Page No.	Street	House Number	Dwelling Number (1)	Family Number (2)	Name of every person whose place of abode on 1 June 1900 was in this family (3)	Relationship to head of family (4)	Color (5)	Sex (6)	Birth Date Month (7)	Birth Date Year (7)	Age (8)	Marital status (9)	# Years married (10)	Mother of how many children? (11)	# of these children living (12)	Birthplace of: This Person (13)	Birthplace of: This Person's Father (14)	Birthplace of: This Person's Mother (15)	Year of Immigration (16)	# Years in U.S. (17)	Naturalized Citizen (18)	Occupation of every person 10 & older (19)	# months not employed (20)	# months in school (21)	Education: Can read (22)	Education: Can write (23)	Education: Speaks English (24)	Owned or rented (25)	Owned free of mortgage (26)	Farm or house (27)	No. of farm schedule (28)

From *Unpuzzling Your Past* by Emily Anne Croom, Betterway Publications, Inc.

1910 CENSUS

Local Community _____

Ward _____

Enumerator _____

State _____

Supervisor's District No. _____

Enumeration District No. _____

County _____

Date Census Taken _____

Page No.	Street	House No. / Dwelling No.	Family No.	Name of each person whose place of abode on 15 April 1910 was in this family	Relationship	Sex	Color	Age	Marital Status	# Years—Present Marriage	Mother of how many children?	# living children	Birthplace of			Year of Immigration	Naturalized or alien?	Speaks English? If not, give name of language.	Profession or Occupation & nature of business		Employer or Wage Earner or Working on Own Account	Out of work 15 April 1910?	# weeks out of work in 1909	Can read	Can write	School since 1 September 1909	Owned / rented	Owned free of mortgage	Farm or house	No. on farm schedule	Civil War Veteran	Blind	Deaf & dumb
		1	2	3	4	5	6	7	8	9	10	11	This Person 12	Father 13	Mother 14	15	16	17	18	19	20	21	22	23	24	25	26	27	28	29	30	31	32

From *Unpuzzling Your Past* by Emily Anne Croom, Betterway Publications, Inc.

Sources for Genealogical Forms and Supplies

The Everton Publishers, Inc.
P.O. Box 368
Logan, UT 84321

Genealogical Books in Print
6818 Lois Drive
Springfield, VA 22150

National Genealogical Society
4527 Seventeenth Street North
Arlington, VA 22207

Suggested Teacher Supplementary Class Material

Chapter 1: A story of one of your ancestors to share with the class.

Chapters 2-5: Each student can use a looseleaf binder (the inexpensive ones with poster board covers are fine) to hold a pedigree chart, sixteen family group sheets, and plain sheets of paper.

Chapters 6-7: "Where to Write for Vital Records" (Publication #017-022-010089; $1.50; Superintendent of Documents, Government Printing Office, Washington, DC 20402.)

The Handy Book for Genealogists, 7th edition. (Logan, UT: The Everton Publishers, Inc., 1981).

Chapter 9: A letter to your state archives, library, and/or historical society as you begin the series of classes should yield some useful information about specific genealogical collections available for research within your state.

Once you have located the genealogy collection for your state, the librarian there should be able to help you with titles to use for the last three classes.

Chapter 10: *Guide to Genealogical Research in the National Archives.* (Washington: National Archives and Records Service, 1982).

A copy of a published military service list for your state.

A copy of a census index for your state or a published census such as the 1790 Census.

Chapters 11-12: A local town, city, or county history.

A published family genealogy.

A published set of records or index to some records for your area.

A published directory for research in your area, e.g. *The Genealogist's Handbook for New England Research.* New England Library Association, 1981.

The Genealogical Helper. Single copy, $4.50. (The Everton Publishers, Inc., P.O. Box 368, Logan, UT 84321).

Bibliography

There are many genealogy books available. Any bookstore will probably have at least one or two. Listed here are two "classics" of the field (Doane and Greenwood), along with several other special titles. This list is only to help you branch out. After working with genealogy for a while, you'll be able to select additional books on your own.

Croom, Emily Anne. *Unpuzzling Your Past: A Basic Guide to Genealogy.* 2nd edition. (Crozet, VA: Betterway Publications, Inc., 1989). This is an excellent second book for you to move on to as you continue your research. The author includes samples of more advanced information you can use about letter writing, about collecting unusual information, and about putting all the information you find together.

Doane, Gilbert H. and Bell, James B. *Searching for Your Ancestors: The How and Why of Genealogy.* (Boston: The New England Historical Genealogical Society, 1980.) This is one of the original genealogy books and is considered a classic.

The Genealogist's Handbook for New England Research. (New England Library Association, 1981). I list this only as a sample of a publication you should look for in your research area. By now, some sort of guide is available for researching just about anywhere.

Greenwood, Val D. *The Researcher's Guide to American Genealogy.* (Baltimore: Genealogical Publishing Company, Inc., 1978). This is the most scholarly of all the genealogy books. It has the most answers to your questions, but it is not light reading.

Guide to Genealogical Research in the National Archives. (Washington: National Archives and Records Service, 1982). This is the best source for information about national records. Along with describing all of the records in the National Archives, it includes samples of many of them, so you can see them for yourself.

The Handy Book for Genealogists. 7th edition. (Logan, UT: The Everton Publishers, Inc., 1981). This is a genealogist's reference book for finding the location of all local records and is a great place to start your research when you move away from family sources of information.

Helmbold, F. Wilbur. *Tracing Your Ancestry.* (Birmingham, AL: Oxmoor Press, 1976). I include this book because it is one of the easiest to use, and it is a good move-up book when you feel you need to know more. There is also a companion *Logbook* which has all sorts of forms for use in your research.

Index